www.rockislandbooks.com

Visit our website to purchase books and preview upcoming titles.

**Contact us at:
books@rockisland.com**

THE LIVING WORD in 3D

Contents

Matthew 11:25,26

At that time Jesus answered and said,

I thank thee, O Father, Lord of heaven and

earth, because thou hast hid these things from

the wise and prudent, and hast revealed them

unto babes. Even so, Father: for so it seemed

good in thy sight.

To my wife, JoAnn.
Without her encouragement
this never would
have happened

The Scarlet Thread

Foreword

Hide and Seek

I believe God hides things from those who approach Him in unbelief. God declares this to be the case without apology.

Jesus thanked God for being the God who both hides and reveals.

Man's mind is already darkened as a result of his own sin and rebellion.

God not only darkens and hides but He also enlightens.

Is it really that surprising that the Author who discloses His mind – and puts to pen His divine purposes – would also act as host and then guide all who are beckoned to read His work and understand its mysteries?

Our prayer continues from the moment of repentance and faith to the moment when the last breath of Earth's stale air is exhausted from our lungs, *Lord reveal yourself to me!*

I find it interesting that the condition in which the Earth found itself when God began the recreation that put things right again is the *same* condition in which Man finds himself before the fulfillment of God's promise: That His word having gone forth would not come back void.

In other words, it is the Word who reconstructs the fallen mind, and fills the once dead soul. It is Christ who enters and once again makes it a habitable place for the Creator to reside. – C.J. Lovik

Many Ancient Mysteries, One Timeless Message

The key to understanding this book

THE LIVING WORD IN 3D examines a code that was embedded in Semitic writing at its very beginning.

The Hebrew language has three overlapping layers that make it unique among all other languages. Chinese has two layers, conventional usage and pictographic. Greek has two layers, conventional and numeric. Only Hebrew has, and has always had, all three:

1. Conventional (common script form)
2. Pictographic
3. Numeric

The Hebrew language combines these three layers to create a unified message of revelation. Each contains either confirmation of the historical Hebrew meaning or in many cases it shines a light on a larger underlying truth that God wants repeated and magnified. The key to understanding the three layers of meaning in the Hebrew aleph-beyt is to explore all three within the contextual boundaries each has, while paying special attention to the clear historical meaning which God clearly put before us as His primary method of revealing truth to Mankind.

Those who previewed parts of this work prior to publication have all reported the same thing: it deepened their faith and increased their love for both the Savior and his Word. That is the fruit we seek, not secret knowledge. It is truly amazing, as readers of THE LIVING WORD IN 3D will discover.

— C.J. LOVIK

Chapter 1: A JOURNEY

Your Invitation . . .

You are invited to join me on a journey that is designed to elicit wonder as we explore the ancient prophetic text that heralded the first coming of the Messiah

THE Hebrew aleph-beyt is uniquely designed to illuminate our understanding of truth from a divine and eternal perspective.

This illumination occurs in the revelation of ancient prophetic text, also referred to as the Bible, or Scriptures, or the Old Testament.

One of the most important ways that God has chosen to reveal Himself is through the precise words contained in Scriptures.

Through these words, God predicts His sublime and heroic work of self-disclosure – that He would clothe His very words with flesh and introduce Himself as the living Word to a fallen world.

The ancient prophetic Hebrew Scriptures contain a message so important that the Author embedded it into the very letters that compose the words.

And it may surprise you to know that within these very Hebrew letters three languages co-exist, each supporting the other with an architecture that is both sublime and wondrous.

This communication structure stands alone as a self-authenticating and self-identifying code. The code integrates pictographic and numeric meanings into the conventional use of the letters as script.

This code, and its purpose for this divine structure and architecture may be deduced. It is the Almighty's signet ring stamped both upon and within His testimony.

At the appointed time – as revealed precisely in the code – the Word exhibited itself supernaturally and became flesh, creating a seamless connection between the expression of words and the emergence of the Word into human flesh.

He became visible and He dwelt among us. He also became identifiable as to His unique nature and mission.

Anyone enabled supernaturally by His Spirit to receive this message, despite all worldly attempts to obscure the disclosure, will see it.

Cave of the Dead Sea Scrolls, known as Qumran cave 4, one of the caves in which the scrolls were found at the ruins of Khirbet Qumran in the desert of Israel.

Did God create this code in order that the sincere seeker might have no doubt about the otherworldly source and supreme authority of His unique revelation to Mankind? The truth will set you free!

PROPHECY AND THE CATEGORIES OF SCRIPTURE

On the basis of the research I have done, certain conclusions and opinions have been firmly formed. One of those opinions relates to the categorization of Scripture as:

- History
- Hymns
- Poetry
- Wisdom
- Prophecy
- Devotional
- Instructional
- Letters

I have no argument with the premise that the Word of God contains all of these categories. I have, however, come to the conclusion that all the categories listed above both contain and are often subordinate to one exception. That one exception is *prophecy*.

It has been calculated that approximately one third of Scripture is prophetic. After you read this book it is my belief that you will come to the conclusion that prophecy infuses *all* of Scripture, not just a portion of it.

But I am getting ahead of myself. It is only fair that I tell you ahead of time that I am a biblical literalist. So if you imagine that I will reconcile the above provocative statement by means of allegory, you would be mistaken.

That is not to say that God has not chosen to reveal much through that literary lens, only that I will not abuse that method in order to beat and fit Scriptures into any preconceived category.

The Scriptures do not need any assistance from me, and as best as I am able, it is my sincere and prayerful duty to allow the God-breathed Word to speak without human interference.

Can I accomplish this goal? Of course not! That does not mean I will not try. Above all else I want you to know what God has revealed.

THE TOOLS FOR THE STUDY OF SCRIPTURE

Lets begin by considering the words of the prophet Jeremiah as recorded in the ancient prophetic text.

Jeremiah 9:23
Thus saith the LORD, Let not the wise man glory in his wisdom, neither let the mighty man glory in his might, let not the rich man glory in his riches:
24: But let him that glorieth, glory in this, that he understandeth and knoweth me . . . "

It is not the purpose of this book to teach you the methods I used to discover the revelations contained in the language embedded in the ancient Hebrew text. Nor is it my purpose to hide those methods.

At the time the text was first written, a Hebrew child who had learned to read could understand it with ease. He might not have understood what it all meant, since the unfolding mystery of God's redemptive plan was just that, a mystery.

Since I am not a Hebrew, you will understand that when it comes to this study I am not nearly as bright as a Hebrew child who lived during the time of Moses. It has taken me several years of intense study and much prayer to reach the point where I can confidently interpret the layered language of pictures and numbers contained in the Hebrew Scriptures.

Trying to teach that method and at the same time disclosing the information that is revealed is simply too confusing and time consuming a task for one book. A brief explanation, including some abbreviated charts and study tools designed to give you confidence that the methods being used are easily replicated, reasonable and reliable is included in the upcoming pages.

THE METHOD

The following is a brief outline of the data used and the methods employed to extract the hidden messages in both the pictorial and numeric letters of the ancient Hebrew Scriptures. I have decided to present this information as a list followed by a couple of tables.

1. The ancient Hebrew Scriptures were given by God, letter by letter, to Moses.

2. Each of the ancient Hebrew letters was originally a picture drawn as a logogram or ideogram in a form familiar to the Hebrews at the time. For example the first letter, aleph, was a symbol representing an ox.

3. Each of the ancient Hebrew letters was also a number that had a meaning based on how it was used in Scripture. It was an enclosed system – the numbers had a meaning based on how they were used in the Scriptures alone and relied on no other source of information.

4. The meanings of the pictures and the numbers are connected with the word that is being expressed and the context of that word in a sentence.

5. The picture connected with each letter anchors the meaning of the word in something tangible that cannot be changed with the passage of time.

6. The same holds true for the numbers. This is why the Hebrew text found in the Dead Sea Scrolls that are thousands of years old can be read today by anyone who knows the Hebrew language.

GOD HAS ANCHORED THE MEANING OF HEBREW WORDS IN PICTURES

This serves many purposes, one of which is to keep the meaning of words from drifting, as they do in all other languages. Could you read an English document only 500 years old? I think not!

The tables on the next pages are presented so that you may have some context for understanding the pictographic and numeric meanings.

This does not mean that you will immediately understand how this is being done, although careful and curious readers will soon figure it out. The Western mind does not easily organize information that was written in a foreign language and context.

TRANSPOSITIONS

One of the most difficult hurdles Western readers will face is the transposition of words when translating from Hebrew to English. For example, the first four words in Genesis 1:1 reads as follows in Hebrew "In beginning He created Elohim the Heavens."

Think about that for a minute. Did "He" create "God"? Is Elohim "the Heavens?" No.

Hebrew is written and read from right to left. Hebrew is written with no spaces between the letters or words, no periods, no clearly marked paragraphs. Hebrew has no past, present or future tense. This is only slightly challenging compared to the real difficulty that the Western mind has when it encounters the sentence structure of the Hebrew language.

If you have ever read a Hebrew Interlinear then you understand the difficulty in translating Hebrew to English. The direct literal translation of Hebrew in English seems at first to be clumsy, confusing and perplexing. Our minds stumble as we juggle the words so that they make sense to us.

There is a mystery in the perplexity of the Hebrew language that I am going to reveal.

> The Greek/Western language is a *noun- first* language. This is a reflection of our mind set.

> The Hebrew is a *verb-first* language. This is a reflection of God's mind.

The theological implications of this are enormous if you take the time to give it some thought. It would require a very large book to explore all the implications of the unique Hebrew language.

A few of the technical riddles of the language are solved when you understand that in order to make Hebrew comprehensible for the English mind, the verb and the noun need to be transposed. The confusion in the Western mind clears up when the verb and the noun are transposed.

A larger mystery looms. Why did God express himself in a way that seems backwards to the Western mind? Time does not permit me to answer that question fully so I will leave you with one nugget to meditate upon.

Why does God emphasize the *verb* instead of the *noun*? The answer is breathtaking. Let me make this personal for you. God is more interested in what you are *becoming* (verb) rather than what you are *now* (noun).

If you understand this you have experienced the unveiling of one of the small mysteries that will help you understand the mind of God. Obviously none of us are going to plumb the depths of God's mind, but that should not keep us from wanting to know His mind based on what He purposely reveals about Himself.

YESHUA HA-MASHIACH A.K.A. JESUS THE CHRIST

The name of Jesus in the Hebrew language is Yeshua. It is true that this name holds mysteries and meaning not present in the English translation of the name of Jesus. That fact does not diminish the power and glory that is in the name of Jesus the Christ.

God has revealed his Son to the nations in their own languages. Yeshua and Jesus are the same person. Ha-Mashiach and the Christ are the same title.

You will notice that we use the Hebrew and the English name of our Lord Jesus. This is meant to be instructive and is not in any way meant to be censorious. We encourage all our English speaking friends and neighbors to call upon the precious name of the Lord Jesus Christ. Others may wish to call upon the name of Yeshua Ha-Mashiach!

We embrace all who worship the Son of God and make no distinction between His name in Hebrew, English, Greek, Spanish, or any other translation of Yeshua Ha-Mashiach.

The Hebrew Aleph-Beyt . . .

Letter	Name and pronunciation	Ancient pictogram and its meaning		Translation of the pictogram	Numeric meaning
א	**Aleph** *aw'-lef*	ox, bull		God the Father, deity, strength, leader, first	1
ב	**Beyt** *bayth*	tent, house		Son of God, household, family, second	2
ג	**Gimel** *ghee'-mel*	camel		Holy Spirit, to lift up, benefit, pride	3
ד	**Dalet** *daw'-let*	door		pathway, to enter, doorway	4
ה	**Hey** *hay*	behold		to behold, to look, to reveal	5
ו	**Vav** *vawv*	iron nail, wooden hook		to add, to secure, to fasten together	6
ז	**Zayin** *zah'-yin*	weapon		cut, to cut off, sever	7
ח	**Chet** *khayth*	fence, inner room		private, separate, fenced off area, sanctuary	8
ט	**Tet** *tayt*	snake, surround		to surround, twist, entwine, entangle	9
י	**Yood** *yode*	hand		a work, a deed, to make something	10
כ/ך	**Kaf** *caf*	palm		to cover, to open, to allow	11/20

. . . and its many meanings

Letter	Name and pronunciation		Ancient pictogram and its meaning		Translation of the pictogram	Numeric meaning
ל	**Lamed**	law'-med		staff	to control, to have authority over, tongue	12/30
מ/ם	**Mem**	mame		water	water, liquid, massive, chaos, raging	13/40
נ/ן	**Noon**	noon		fish	activity, life	14/50
ס	**Samech**	saw'-mek		prop	to support, prop up, twist slowly, turn	15/60
ע	**Ayin**	ah'-yin		eye	to see, to know, to experience, to understand	16/70
פ/ף	**Pey**	pay		mouth	to speak, a word, to open	17/80
צ/ץ	**Tsade**	tsaw-day'		fishhook	to catch, to strongly desire, to crave, to need	18/90
ק	**Qoof**	cofe		back of the head	behind, the last, the least	19/100
ר	**Reysh**	raysh		head	the head person, the prince, the head, the highest	20/200
ש/שׂ	**Seen** / **Sheen**	sin / shyn		teeth	sharp, to consume, to destroy, the Name of God	21/300
ת	**Tav**	tawv		sign	to seal, to cove-nant or make an agreement	22/400

* *when more than one number is shown, the first number is its place number in the aleph bety.*
The second number is its value.

The Numbers . . .

EACH HEBREW LETTER IS ALSO A NUMBER

Hebrew numbers have a meaning anchored in how they are used in Scripture. Numbers that seemed to only hint at a meaning have become clearer and crisper as the ancient prophetic text unfolded in time and space. Our vantage point based on the unfolding of the prophetic word combined with the historical record gives us a perspective that the ancients could only dream about. What was sealed up for the last days and could not be understood by even Daniel himself is now so clear that a child can grasp and grapple with it. The unfolding revelation has unfolded! Some of the numbers used in Scripture have a meanings rooted in how those numbers where used in the measurements of the Temple. New Testament believers understand that the Temple was a type and shadow of the Lord Jesus Christ. The shadows and types hidden in the Temple come into bold relief as you read the revelations regarding Jesus the Christ contained in the New Testament. Christians who have an interest in understanding the significance of numbers would be well served by adding the following two books to their library: *Number in Scripture, Its Supernatural Design and Spiritual Significance* written by E. W. Bullinger. *Biblical Mathematics* written by Ed F. Vallowe. Bullinger's work is 150 years old and still recognized as the authoritative work on biblical numbers. Ed F. Vallowe fills in some of the gaps left by Bullinger. Both books are a must for anyone serious about understanding what numbers mean based on how they are used in the Scriptures.

1	Deity, unity, sufficiency, independence, first, God the Father.
2	Difference (good or evil) division, living word, second, God the Son.
3	Divine perfection, the completion of an order, completeness, solid, substantial, the entirety, God the Holy Spirit.
4	Creation, the world, God's creative works, the fourth thing, first number that can be divided.
5	Grace, God's favor, the Pentateuch, the fifth in an order, divine strength.
6	Man's world, enmity with God, weakness of Man, manifestation of sin, evils of Satan, falling short, preservation, imperfection, Man without God, labor, sorrow, secular completeness, sixth.
7	Spiritual perfection, completeness, resurrection.
8	Eternality, new creation, first in a new series, new birth, new beginnings.
9	Conclusion of a matter, last of all digits, summation of Man's works, judgment of Man, wrath, fruit of the Spirit, divine completeness from the father.
10	Ordinal perfection, completion and perfection of a divine order or sequence of ordinances, numbers or specific events, usually within reference to time. Testimony, the law of Moses, responsibility to the law.

11	Judgement, disorder, deliberate manifestation of chaos and disorganization, imperfection, the subversion of an order designed to bring about Confusion. Consequences of deliberate rebellion againt God's authority.
12	Governmental perfection. The establishment of a perfect order which can only come about as a result of divine intervention and can only be maintained by divine governance and supervision.
13	Apostasy, depravity and rebellion, ill omen, corruption, defection, revolution, depravity.
14	Deliverance, salvation, double perfection (2x7).
15	Grace (3x5), brought about by the energy of divine grace and associated with perfect timing or a perfect time) 8+7 (resurrection being a special mark of the energy of divine grace issuing in glory). Rest.
16	Love.
17	Seventh number in a series (1,3,5,7,11,13,17). Union of spiritual perfection plus ordinal perfection, perfection of spiritual order; victory.
18	Bondage.
19	Faith, perfection of divine order connected with judgment (10+9).
20	Redemption, 10x2 = concentrated meaning of ordinal perfection. Expectancy.
21	Exceeding sinfulness of sin, 3-7's, ultimate spiritual perfection.
22	Light, number of letters in Hebrew aleph-beyt so 22 can have the idea of the complete word.
23	Death.
24	The priesthood; 12x2 (concentrated meaning perfection of government).
25	Repentance, intercession, the forgiveness of sins.
26	The Gospel of Christ, total letter count for YHVH is 26.
27	Preaching of the Gospel, cube of 3, divine perfection connected with judgment.
28	4x7 - creation and spiritual perfection. Eternal life.
29	Departure, going away.

30	Blood of Christ, dedication, 3x10 (high degree of the perfection of divine order as marking the right moment).
31	Number of Deity, aleph (1) lamed (12-30) 1+30 =31, offspring.
32	Covenant.
33	Promise.
34	Naming of a son.
35	Hope.
36	Enemy.
37	The word of our Father.
38	Slavery.
39	Disease.
40	Trials, probation, testings, chastisement (not judgment) 5x8 – action of grace (revival, renewal) 4x10 – renewed or extended rule or dominion.
42	Israel's oppression, 1st advent, Antichrist (42 months 30x42=1260), 6x7 – connection between Christ and Antichrist, between Man and Spirit of God.
44	Judgment of the world 4x11 = 44, creation multiplies its corruption and sinfulness to the overflowing of the cup.
45	Preservation, judgement folllowed by grace.
50	Holy Spirit, Pentecost, jubilee, deliverance followed by rest.
51	Divine revelation.
60	Pride.
65	Apostacy and judgment (Ephraim).
66	Idol worship.
70	Punishment and restoration of Israel, universality, 7x10 perfect spiritual order carried out with all spiritual power and significance.

90	Signifies the end of a series, the finality of a period. The time when something has reached it's conclusion, is evaluated or judged and a new series begins. Nine is the last digit before a new number series begins.
100	Election, children of the promise.
119	Spiritual perfection and victory 7x17=119, the resurrection day, Lord's Day.
120	Divine period (appointed time) of probation.
144	The Spirit guided life.
200	Man's insufficiency, God's sufficiency.
300	Divine spiritual order brought about by a divine act of restoration. Restoration which can only follow a gracious perfect blood sacrifice which puts an end to Man's sin and thus restores Man to the fellowship and relationship with God. Victory over God's enemies and over sin brought about by supernatural means.
400	Divinely perfected period of time (8x50, or eight unique Jubilees added together).
600	Warfare.
666	The number of the beast Antichrist, the perfection of imperfection, culmination of human pride, independence from God, opposition to his Christ.
700	Perfect period of rest brought about at exactly the right time by the sovereign ordinances of God.
777	The trinity of sevens signifies spiritual perfection multiplied in both power and completeness resulting in a Rest found only in Yeshua Ha-Mashiach.
888	The trinity of eights summed up in the first resurrection of the saints, the tree of life and the New Beginning brought about by the divine work of the Holy Spirit.
1,000	Divine completeness and Father's glory.
4,000	Salvation of the world through the blood of the Lamb, those who chose between Christ and Antichrist.
6,000	Deception of Antichrist, second Advent.
7,000	Final judgment followed by millenial reign of Yeshua Ha-Mashiach as Jesus the Christ.

Chapter 2: IN THE BEGINNING

The 3D Exposition of Genesis

Our purpose is to discover and reveal the picture and number messages hidden in plain sight and embedded in the 28 letters that make up Genesis 1:1

We'll start with a literal Hebrew to English translaton. Most of you recognize these as the very first words in the Torah.

Genesis 1:1
In the beginning God created the heaven and the earth.

Would it surprise you that a wealth of information is embedded into the first words of the Hebrew Scripture just waiting to be discovered? Let's begin our search. The first word in the ancient prophetic text literally means "in beginning," and much can be inferred by the missing "the," which is nowhere present in the original disclosure of Scripture. We will discuss this in a future chapter.

The literal meaning of the first Hebrew word of the bible is "in beginning." Most English versions of the Bible translate the first Hebrew word found in the Scriptures as "in the beginning." Most Hebrew language scholars agree that it would be better simply to translate it into English as "in *a* beginning" instead of "in *the* beginning." Just to be very clear: The literal translation of the Hebrew word b-rashith, according to the Westmin-ster Leningrad Codex Authorized Version Hebrew to English Interlinear, is "in beginning."

IN BEGINNING

The conventional translation is concise. As it is the first word in the first book of the ancient Hebrew Scriptures let's give it the special attention it deserves.

Could it be that this word "in beginning" is the first stepping-stone that leads us to the enfolding path or doorway to revelation that, once embraced by faith, leads to life itself?

What happens if this fundamental truth contained in the word "in beginning" is denied? I believe the answer to the question is that denial results in nothing short of judicial blindness! Deny the initial authorship of all things proceeding from the spoken Word of God and darkness follows.

Earth before God began his Re-Creation was described as "without form and void." Literal translations of the Hebrew words for "without form" and "void" are tohu bohu. Those Hebrew

Hebrew spelling of verse

א. בראשית ברא אלהים
את השמים ואת הארץ

Hebrew pronunciation of verse

Be•re•shéet ba•ra Elohím et ha•sha•má•yim ve•et ha•á•retz

English translation of verse

(Left to right) English   *(Right to left) Hebrew*

1. In the Beginning God created the heaven and earth

א. בראשית ברא אלהים
את השמים ואת הארץ

The first word
b - rashith – *pronounced Be•re•shéet*

ברא שית

Tav	Yood	Sheen	Aleph	Reysh	Beyt
400	10	300	1	200	2

English translation of b-rashith: English/Hebrew literal translation:
In the Beginning   **In Beginning**

words literally mean chaotic and un-inhabitable.

I think it is interesting that we are told that God's Word when it goes forth will not return *void*. Another way of saying this would be that God's Word when it goes forth creates a habitable place.

In other words, it is the Word that reconstructs the fallen mind and fills the once dead soul. It is Christ who enters and once again makes it a habitable place for the Creator to reside.

If you have put your faith in Yeshua Ha-Mashiach then you have become a place of habitation for Him, and He promises to abide forever more within you. It is this entry by the Creator into the formally vacant and formless place that is the guarantee of your eternal connection with the King of Heaven. Once He enters in, He promises never to depart. You have become a temple in which God permanently takes up residence. You are His new creation.

The one who created all things has expressed His displeasure with those who deny His preeminent creative power, or hide the truth of it, or deny it, or rebel against it. Read Romans 1.

It can then be added for emphasis that the Golden Rule of biblical interpretation is only golden to those who embrace the Word of God with faith and seek to understand it with reverence and humility. With this firmly in mind let us approach the first two words in Holy Scripture for the purpose of discovering what might be revealed in plain sight.

PICTOGRAPHIC MEANING OF THE HEBREW WORD "IN BEGINNING"

The second language we will explore is expressed in pictures. So let's look at the pictographic meaning of the first two words of the ancient Hebrew Scriptures.

Reysh Beyt

THE FIRST TWO LETTERS

The first two letters of the word "beginning" are beyt and reysh. The pictogram for beyt is the picture of a tent or a house. The pictogram for reysh is the picture of the head or highest person.

It may help you to understand that abba (father) is written with two Hebrew letters – the aleph and the beyt. Abba is the pictogram of the strong leader (aleph) of the tent or house (beyt). So it follows that the strong leader of the house is the father. The highest person or head that comes out of the house or tent is the son. The word for "the son" translated "bar" is beyt reysh. Most of us have heard of the term Bar Mitzvah. We know it is something that happens to a Jewish boy when he is 13 years old. But do you know what the word Bar Mitzvah means? It means "The son of the covenant." We also find this word "bar" in the New Testament:

> **Matthew 16:17**
> And Jesus answered and said unto him; blessed art thou; Simon Barjona: for flesh and blood hath not revealed *it* unto thee; but my Father; which is in heaven.

> **Acts 13:6**
> And when they had gone through the isle unto Patmos, they found a certain sorcerer, a false prophet, a Jew; whose name *was* Barjesus:

In the Gospel of Matthew, Simon Barjona is the son of Jona. In Acts of the Holy Spirit the Jewish false prophet BarJesus was the son of Jesus (not Jesus Christ obviously). So, the conventional meaning of bar is "The Son." As a pictogram, bar is viewed as the highest person coming out of the house or tent.

Aleph

THE THIRD LETTER: ALEPH

Aleph, the third letter in the word "in beginning," is pictured as an ox. We just learned how this letter is used to construct the word "Abba." We now understand that aleph means the strong leader. Aleph is also the letter that on many occasions is the first letter in the revelation of the names of God, including:

- Elohim (aleph/lamed/hey/yod/mem)
- El
- Adonai
- and others.

Aleph also means one. It has the meaning of indivisible and unique. Finally aleph, as it is used in Hebrew words, is often the letter that represents God.

Sheen

THE FOURTH LETTER

Sheen is the picture of teeth. Sheen has the meaning of:

- Sharp
- To Press Against
- To Devour
- To Destroy

Yood

THE FIFTH LETTER

Yood is the picture of an arm and hand. Yood has the meaning of accomplishing a deed with a hand. The picture is of a bare arm flexing to do a work or task.

Tav

THE FINAL LETTER

Tav is the picture of crossed sticks or a cross. Tav has the meaning of:
- A sign or mark
- Monument
- Covenant

So let's see what pictographic message is embedded in the Hebrew word "in beginning."

PUTTING THE SIX PICTURES TOGETHER

Remember the place of prominence is reserved for the first, so the message contained in the pictorial meaning of the Hebrew word "in beginning" must be pretty important. And guess what? *It is.*

Before we decipher the pictographic message embedded in the word "in beginning," let's remind ourselves of something Yeshua (Jesus) said as reported by John the Jewish fisherman and follower of Yeshua.

> **John 5:39**
> Search the scriptures; for in them ye think ye have eternal life: and they are they which testify of me."

What follows, I believe, is the Creator's watermark – His seal of authenticity. Think of it as the Monarch of the Universe's ring stamped into the wax of Man's heart and mind, making a unique and indelible impression.

The King of the heavens has filled the Cosmos with His testimony and His orderly plan for the

PICTOGRAPHIC MEANINGS OF THE HEBREW WORD "IN BEGINNING"

Beyt: house tent, family, Son of God – **Tent-House**

Reysh: a person, the prince, the head, the highest – **Head**

Aleph: strong leader, first, God the Father – **Ox**

Sheen: to consume, to destroy, to press against – **Teeth**

Yood: work, a deed, to make – **Hand**

Tav: to seal, to covenant, a sign, crossed sticks – **Cross**

redemption of man – a message that, at its very heart, is about His only begotten Son and the work of His hands for the benefit of His fallen creation.

Should we really be surprised that the One who spoke the worlds into existence should have the skill to infuse His message into every letter of His revelation to Man?

Would we use a telescope to marvel at the wonders of God's redemptive plan pictured in the heavens and deny the efficiency of a microscope to uncover the same miracle? *Of course not.*

Is this a holy hologram? Is it the revelation inside the revelation? Are we looking at the portrait of the Yeshua Ha-Mashiach in which the larger portrait is made up of pixels that are also stamped with the same portrait?

If you remove even a large portion of the bigger picture is the exact replica of the entire work preserved in the pieces left behind?

I believe so! What a Savior!

LOOK AT THE PICTURE MESSAGE HIDDEN IN THE FIRST SIX HEBREW LETTERS OF "IN THE BEGINNING":

> The Son of God pressed by his own hand to a cross.

Now suppose that God wanted to find a place to put before Man the most important revelation He had for Adam's fallen race. Don't you think He might hide it in plain sight so that all who found it would discover His very heartbeat and marvel at the divine ingenuity that not only published the message but also did it in such a way that its author and origin was undeniable.

Isn't this where you would put the message above all messages – a message to which all other revelations are subordinate?

Is it not reasonable that this special place in the Word would be reserved for the revelation above all other revelations – the biggest surprise man has ever encountered – that God became a man and took upon Himself our degradation and iniquity and paid the penalty for it on a wooden tree so that we might escape the wrath of God and enter into the presence of the Heavenly Father as much beloved children, not rebellious criminals lined up for a death sentence.

Are we really surprised that God would inscribe his most awesome work with the name of Yeshua Ha-Mashiach? Isn't this where He would encode His most important message on the billboard of the first words in His Revelation? Guess what. He did! Words fail! Simply contemplate the wonder of this revelation and worship your Savior!

Let this revelation soak into your soul that the Lord God, our Savior Yeshua Ha-Mashiach, revealed His redemptive purpose in the very first words of Holy Writ. Can there be any doubt that the Messiah, Yeshua Ha-Mashiach, is hidden in plain sight inside the letters of the Hebrew aleph-beyt? But wait, there is more.

WHAT'S UNDER THE NUMBERS?

Figuring out the numbers in the Hebrew word "in beginning" is simple. Each Hebrew letter is also a number.

We simply treat the letters as if they are numbers. On the table next page, I have put the numeric value next to each Hebrew letter that comprises the word "in beginning:"

> In the West, numbers and letters are different. In Hebrew they are the same – so I have added the Western rendition of the Hebrew numbers and placed them below the Hebrew number/letter in order that you might more easily understand the Hebrew numeric system.

The meaning of the numbers is based on how they are used in Scripture.

I am relying on major works on this topic that have already been accomplished by E.W. Bullinger in his book *Number In Scripture: Its Supernatural Design and Spiritual Significance* and Dr. Ed F. Vallowe's book titled Biblical Mathematics: *The Keys to Scripture Numerics.*

Let's look at the biblical and spiritual significance of the six numbers that make up the word "in beginning."

PROPHETIC TIME STAMP ANNOUNCING THE COMING MESSIAH?

The twin numbers that jumped out at me first were yood and tav.

ת   י

Tav   Yood

400   10

Among the list of six letter/numbers that comprise the Hebrew word "in beginning" these are the only numbers that have to do with time. Yood (10) is one of four perfect numbers in the Hebrew aleph-beyt.

Ten has the meaning of ordinal perfection. But just what exactly does ordinal perfection mean? The word ordinal implies a sequence of numbers of events that happen in a specific order.

Ordinal perfection means that God has a sequence of numbers or events that will unfold in a preordained order, accomplishing His purpose perfectly and completely as designed without interruption or deviation.

> The number yood (10) ten signifies completion of a sequence. The number tav (400) is

28

NUMERIC MEANINGS OF THE HEBREW WORD "IN BEGINNING"

2	ב	**Beyt:** Difference (good or evil), division, living word, second, God the Son.
200	ר	**Reysh:** Man's insufficiency, God's Sufficiency
1	א	**Aleph:** Deity, unity, sufficiency, independence, the first, God the Father.
300	ש	**Sheen:** Victory over evil, victory of God over Satan. Symbolizes those who put their faith and trust in the crucified and risen Christ.
10	י	**Yood:** Ordinal perfection, perfection of divine order, completeness of order.
400	ת	**Tav:** Divinely perfected period of time (8x50 or eight unique jubilee's added together)

a divinely ordered period of time based on the accomplishment of an eternal purpose that will bring about a new beginning or new birth. The number is comprised of eight non-sequential Jubilees of 50 years each.

Jubilees signify deliverance from bondage and debt. Eight signifies a new beginning or new birth, and eternity.

Eight 50-year Jubilees signifies that this period of divinely appointed time has been elevated in its meaning to the realm of the eternal. So whatever it is that is going to happen during and upon the completion of this 400-year period has eternal significance.

Are the two Hebrew letters together – yood and tav – a clue meant to inform the reader that there is a divinely appointed time that will impact our eternity? If we calculate that period of time by counting ten periods of time that are 400 years each have we solved a mystery? Perhaps.

There is no question that yood and tav put togeth-er have to do with a divinely appointed period of time. The question is: *What* divinely appointed period of time?

Is God communicating the fact that ten epochs of 400 years will unfold in human history and at the completion of this preordained time period something amazing is going to happen?

To put the question another way: Do the first words in the first book of the Bible that contain two number/letters reveal a prophecy that there is a countdown of 4,000 years from the first day of creation as recorded in the book of Genesis? Are we to understand that during that period of time God has ordained a sequence of events that will unfold and in the fullness of that 4,000-year epoch it will bring about deliverance from bondage and debt? How many years passed between the six days of creation and the birth of Jesus Christ?

James Usher, after examining the Biblical genealogical record, placed the date of the first day of creation on the night before October 23, 4004 B.C. While I may have a few questions about the precision of Bishop Ushers estimate, I do not

question the accuracy of his calculation based on the genealogical record, as it records the passage of time from day one of creation to the birth of Christ.

According to man's best modern research, Jesus of Nazareth was born sometime between 2 B.C. and 1 A.D. So that would put about 4,000 years between the creation of the world and the birth of Jesus Christ. Did God prophetically reveal from day one that deliverance would be needed and would arrive on schedule exactly 4,000 years from the first day of the creation account? One thing is for certain: Deliverance arrived in the person of Yeshua Ha-Mashiach right on God's prophetic calendar, 4,000 years from day one. *Coincidence?*

THE NEXT NUMBERS

The next two numbers that arrested my attention were the number/letters aleph and reysh.

Aleph	Reysh
1	200

Reysh, 200, is the number of insufficiency. Aleph, 1, is the number of sufficiency. Man is insufficient. But what Man cannot accomplish God the Father, who is all sufficient, can. Obviously the deliverance that God had forecast and ordained is not going to happen without divine intervention. More about this later.

THE FINAL NUMBERS

The next number that got my attention is the number sheen, 300.

Sheen
300

This number contains the message that God is

going to accomplish victory over evil and Satan. But how will this transpire?

Beyt
2

The number beyt (2) is the answer. Among other meanings, one of the prominent meanings of beyt – and the only one that fits the context of the numeric message – is that God's Son is going to accomplish this by means hinted at in the pictographic meaning of "in beginning."

> The Son of God pressed by his own hand to a cross.

The number sheen fills in the blanks with the following revelation – the number 300, as used in Scripture, symbolizes those who put their faith and trust in the crucified and risen Messiah.

THE MEANING OF THE NUMBERS

Tav, 400. Yood, 10: God has ordained a sequence of events that will unfold over a period of 4,000 years culminating in deliverance and victory over sin and Satan.

Aleph, 1. Reysh, 200: During this period of time God will demonstrate man's insufficiency and His sufficiency.

Sheen, 300. Beyt, 2: Unearned and unexpected salvation will be made sufficient and effective to all those who put their faith and trust in the crucified and risen Messiah.

This concludes the numeric revelation contained in the Hebrew numbers embedded in the Hebrew word "in beginning."

There is one more revelation regarding the word "in beginning" that I have saved for last.

THE PRINCIPLE OF FIRST USE

There is a principle in biblical hermeneutics (fancy name for studying the Bible) called the principle of first use. It points out that the first use of a word in the Scriptures carries with it special importance as a template for understanding how the word should be understood. I have discovered another biblical principle, which I call the *principle of the final word.* As I have investigated hundreds of words, I have discovered that the principle of the final word adds a layer of meaning and significance to the word being studied.

The principle of first use and the principle of the final word are bookends for the context and meaning of a word, often revealing the words deeper theological significance.

Let's investigate the last time in Scripture that the word "beginning" is used. Jesus, speaking of Himself as recorded by the Apostle John, says in the 22nd chapter, the 13th verse of the book of Revelation, "I am Alpha and Omega, the beginning and the end, the first and the last."

Yeshua Ha-Mashiach (Jesus Christ) is the beginning. The beginning is not just the start of something, it is Yeshua. And He is also the Omega, the tav, and the end of all things. Sadly, nothing ends well unless it ends in Him alone. He is the ending that gives life for a new beginning. When this world of sin and sufferings come to an end, a new life of eternal bliss begins if you are found in Him.

John 1:1
In the beginning was the Word, and the Word was with God, and the Word was God.
2. The same was in the beginning with God.
3. All things were made by him; and without him was not any thing made that was made.

4. In him was life; and the life was the light of men.

The implications are staggering. I admit to being incapable of doing anything but scratch the edges of this amazing truth. The mystery of time and space are literally *in* the Son of God. They are His mysteries to reveal and unfold, as He desires.

> The One Who has no beginning has *become* a beginning in order that we might enter into His company and share His bountiful love. The One Who has no beginning and has no end puts an end to all things He once began in order to transport us to a new beginning that He promises has no end.

And why does the promised new beginning have no end? What makes this beginning different from all the beginnings that have an end point? The answer to this question is stunning in its significance.

Consider this: The new beginning, by means I cannot understand, puts us *in* Him and forever *outside* the reach of sin, rebellion and time that starts and stops. He becomes our never-ending beginning, permanently rooted in the fount of life. He becomes the object of all our comings and goings for eternity. In Him we partake of eternal life! How can we neglect so great a Savior?

We have now finished our preliminary study of one word in Scripture and found to our amazement that it contains the scarlet threads of the Gospel, secrets about eternity, secrets about the origin of the universe and a worshipful profile of the Son of God! This should encourage us to go on to the next word with expectancy. Are there treasures in the second word of the Torah lying in plain sight just waiting to be discovered? Please continue reading. I believe you will not be disappointed.

b - rashith – **In Beginning**

Pictographic translation
Complete reference table, pages 16-17

בראשית

ת	י	ש	א	ר	ב
To a Cross	By His Own Hand	Pressed	Of God		The Son

The Son of God Pressed by His Own Hand to a Cross

Numeric translation
Complete reference table, pages 18-21

(2) The Son of God (200) overcomes Man's insufficiency (1) with God's all-sufficiency! Winning a (300) victory over sin and death through a (10) divinely perfected sequence of events that brings about (400) salvation at the divinely appointed time!

The Ancient Mystery in 3d Revealed
As the Scriptures Unfolded in Time

The Son of God fashioned man out of the red earth with his own hands. Those same hands at the appointed time will fashion another creative miracle. Man had rebelled against his Creator and fallen under the curse of sin and death. Man is incapable and unable to achieve his own deliverance. The Son of God mercifully will accomplish what is impossible for man. Only the Son can restore life and bring salvation and restoration. You will know this creative miracle has been accomplished when you see the **Son of God Pressing His Own Hand To a Cross!**

*And he bearing his **cross** went forth into a place called the place of a skull, which is called in the Hebrew Golgotha: John 19:17*

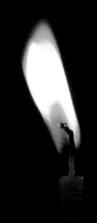

Chapter 3 ~ HE CREATED

בּרא

bra – **He created**

"He" is God

*The common meaning of the Hebrew word
"He created" is easily understood:
Creation is the result of Him!*

"HE" is disclosed as none other than God the Son, the exalted head over all creation. "He" is the highest person who is the first cause of all His creation at the direction of the Father.

The pictogaphic revelation is amazing in its simplicity. The second word in Genesis 1:1 based on the original Hebrew gives us three letters that paint two pictures.

Reysh Beyt

The first two letters sketch the picture of the prince or head man (reysh) coming out of the tent or home (beyt). The Hebrew letters beyt (tent) and reysh (prince) are the same two letters we deciphered the meaning of in chapter two.

The beyt reysh (pronounced "bar" in Hebrew) means "the Son."

So, the first pictogram translation we find in the Hebrew word translated "He created," based on the pictograms represented by the letters beyt and reysh, is *The Son.* The next question is "whose son is he?"

Aleph

The second pictogram translation emerges seamlessly from the third letter in the Hebrew word "He created."

The pictogram for aleph is an ox. The ox has the meaning of the strong leader. It is the first letter in many of the names of God and as the first

Hebrew spelling of verse

א. בראשית ברא אלהים
את השמים ואת הארץ

Hebrew pronunciation of verse

Be•re•shéet ba•ra Elohím et ha•sha•má•yim ve•et ha•á•retz

English translation of verse

(Left to right) English   *(Right to left) Hebrew*

**1. In the Beginning God
created the heaven and earth**

א. בראשית ברא אלהים
את השמים ואת הארץ

---

bra – *pronounced ba•ra*

ברא

Aleph	Reysh	Beyt
1	200	2

PICTOGRAPHIC MEANING OF THE HEBREW WORD "HE CREATED"

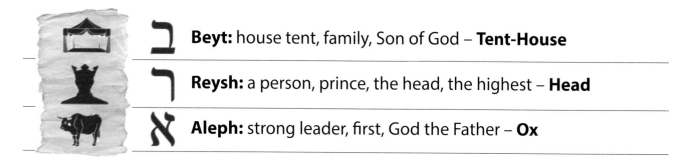

Beyt: house tent, family, Son of God – **Tent-House**

Reysh: a person, prince, the head, the highest – **Head**

Aleph: strong leader, first, God the Father – **Ox**

---

letter of the Hebrew aleph-beyt often represents God. Context is king! There is no question based on the conventional context of the Hebrew word "He created" that the picture we have in view is of the Creator God. The second pictogram is of God!

PICTOGRAPHIC TRANSLATION OF "HE CREATED"

Aleph Reysh Beyt

God the Father, God the Son, God the Holy Spirit

The numeric revelation is just as amazing as the pictographic. It is also eloquently simple.

NUMERIC TRANSLATION OF "HE CREATED"

God the Father is the first. He is all sufficient and completely independent. God the Son is revealed as the second who is one with the Father. The Son reveals the will and purpose of the Father in all His creation. He is the Living Word who spoke all things into existence and according to the testimony of the Father it was all good.

"He" is disclosed as none other than God the Son – the exalted head over all creation.

"He" is the highest person Who is the first cause of all His creation at the direction of the Father

NUMERIC MEANING OF THE HEBREW WORD "HE CREATED"

2	ב	**Beyt:** Difference (good or evil), division, living word, second, God the Son
200	ר	**Reysh:** Man's insufficiency, God's sufficiency
1	א	**Aleph:** Deity, unity, sufficiency, independence, the first, God the Father

37

There is one word that summarizes the numeric meaning of the Hebrew word "He created." That word is *hierarchy*.

We have all heard one of the most common arguments for the design theory or deistic creation model: A man finds a watch and postulates that there must be a watchmaker. And while I can appreciate the illustration, it is fatally flawed as a revelatory concept of creation.

God did not make earth and all that dwells in it, wind it up and set it in nothingness to tick away until the springs wore out. No.

God spoke all that we see into existence, made Man in His image and holding Man in His own hands breathed His life into Man and placed him as His steward over all the earth.

God then regularly had sweet fellowship with His image-bearer, Man, until the image was corrupted by the disobedience of Man at the bidding of an outside antagonist who is hell-bent on destroying anything and everything that brings the Creator glory.

> A watch once wound up requires no further assistance to tick away the minutes, days and decades. In that sense it is free to exercise its designed purpose until the moment it loses the power to do so, and then it simply stops being useful until it is rewound. For an unspecified period of time the watch is sufficient unto itself to accomplish its intended purpose, which is to chronicle the passage of time.

Man was not created like a clock. His purpose requires that he be insufficient on his own, and completely dependent upon the One who created him in His own image and for His own purpose. And what is that purpose? The equation is rather simple. If a thing is insufficient, it lacks something in order to function as it is designed. In a nutshell, Man was designed by God for God. Man's insufficiency was created to be filled by God's sufficiency. *It is really that simple!*

Here is the headline: Man before the Fall was insufficient! That may come as a surprise to some who assume that Man was created perfect. Man was not created perfect. He was created sinless. There is a big difference. Man's perfection was the purpose of the Garden of Eden. If Adam had passed the test, perfection no doubt would have been the reward. But Man failed his probation and plunged all creation into chaos and confusion.

WHAT THE NUMBERS SAY

An all-sufficient God created all things to be subordinate and dependent upon Him. The result of this creative design was to bring glory to the Creator and happiness to the creature. And what is the "final word?" The final occurrence of the word "created" is found in Chapter 10, verses 5-6, as recorded by the Apostle John in the book of Revelation:

> **Revelation 10:5-6**
> 5 And the angel which I saw stand upon the sea and upon the earth lifted up his hand to heaven,
> 6 And sware by him that liveth for ever and ever, who created heaven, and the things that therein are, and the earth, and the things that therein are, and the sea, and the things which are therein, that there should be time no longer:

One day soon, days as we know them will end, along with time as we now experience it. For those who are found in Christ this is going to be a glorious new beginning.

For those who are not found in Christ . . . oh, dear.

bra– **He Created**

Pictographic translation
Complete reference table, pages 16-17

of God   The Son

The Son of God

Numeric translation
Complete reference table, pages 18-21

The Son (of God) overcomes Man's insufficiency
with God's all-sufficency.

The Ancient Mystery in 3d Revealed
As the Scriptures Unfolded in Time

The Insufficiency of Man is displayed in all his thoughts and deeds.
The vast majority of Fallen men in this condition will persist in
attempting to perfect themselves. A very few will cast off all their
vain aspirations of self salvation and humbly Rest in the
All Sufficient Son of God!

*In the beginning was the Word, and the Word was with God,
and the Word was God. John 1:1*

Chapter 4 ~ ELOHIM

elohim

The Trinity in the Letters
Elohim and Divine Architecture

DO you see the Trinity in the first three letters of Elohim? The first clue that Elohim is plural can be found in the final Hebrew letter in the name Elohim.

The final letter is the Hebrew letter mem. In English when we add an "s" to the end of a word it changes it from singular to plural. In Hebrew when you add the Hebrew letter "mem" to the end of a word it changes it from singular to plural. This is just one of many clues that reveal the fact that we are looking at the Triune Creator God.

The second clue can be found in the placement of the name Elohim in the ancient prophetic text. If you look at the above Hebrew translation of Genesis 1:1 you will notice that Elohim is the third word revealed in the original Hebrew.

There is much more!

THE TRIUNE GOD-HEAD REVEALED IN THE FIRST THREE LETTERS OF ELOHIM

ה ל א
Hey Lamed Aleph

God the Father, Son and Holy Spirit

The first letter in the name of Elohim is the Hebrew letter aleph. The pictogram for aleph is an ox. He is the strong leader. The word Father in Hebrew is ABBA. Abba in Hebrew is spelled with two letters, the aleph and the beyt. He is the strong leader of the house. Many of the names and titles of God begin with the letter aleph. Aleph is the first letter in the Hebrew aleph-beyt

Hebrew spelling of verse

א. בראשית ברא אלהים
את השמים ואת הארץ

Hebrew pronunciation of verse

Be•re•shéet ba•ra | Elohím | et ha•sha•má•yim ve•et ha•á•retz

---

English translation of verse

(Left to right) English	*(Right to left) Hebrew*
1. In the Beginning God created the heaven and earth	א. בראשית ברא אלהים את השמים ואת הארץ

---

elohim – *pronounced elohim*

Mem	Yood	Hey	Lamed	Aleph
40	10	5	30	1

PICTOGRAPHIC MEANING OF THE WORD "ELOHIM"

Aleph: strong leader, first, God the Father – **Ox**

Lamed: control, authority, the tongue – **Staff**

Hey: reveal, look – **Behold**

Yood: work, a deed, to make – **Hand**

Mem: liquid, massive, chaos – **Water**

and it is also the first number in the Hebrew number system. If there is one letter in the name of Elohim that represents God the Father it is the first letter of the Hebrew aleph-beyt.

THE SON OF GOD

The second letter in the name of Elohim is the Hebrew letter lamed.

The pictogram for lamed is a staff. When we think of a staff we think of a shepherd and sheep. Does the shepherd's staff bring any person to your mind? Lamed has a meaning that is amazing in this context. Lamed means the person who *speaks* with *authority*. We are told in the New Testament that Jesus spoke with authority and not like the scribes, Pharisees and teachers of the law. Jesus tells us that His sheep hear His authoritative voice and follow Him.

The worlds were spoken into existence by the authoritative word of God. In the gospel of John we learn that the authoritative Word that spoke all the worlds into existence was the living Word Who became flesh and dwelt among men. The authoritative Word is none other that Yeshua Ha-Mashiach, aka Jesus the Christ.

THE HOLY SPIRIT OF GOD

The third letter in the name of Elohim is the Hebrew letter hey.

The pictogram for the Hebrew letter hey is a man lifting up his hands and looking up to the heavens. Hey means to *reveal*. Who is the Revealer? He is none other than the Holy Spirit of God.

A MIGHTY DEED

The fourth letter in the name of Elohim is the Hebrew letter yood. The pictogram for the Hebrew letter yood is a hand doing work. Yood means to accomplish a mighty deed or to do a work. We often speak of God's handiwork and the works of His hands. And that expression is an apt metaphor we can easily understand. But consider that with one exception that we know of all His handiwork was created by means of the spoken Word. Here is the exception:

Genesis 2:7
And the Lord God formed man of the dust of the ground, and breathed into his nostrils the breath of life; and man became a living soul.

Could it be that we have pictured in the fourth letter of the name of Elohim not only that He created Man with His own hands, but also that He is going to do a mighty work on behalf of Mankind. And could it be that the mighty work He is going to do can be pictured by a hand?

STREAMS OF LIVING WATER

The fifth letter in the name of Elohim is the Hebrew letter mem. The pictogram for the Hebrew letter mem is waters. Mem can mean the chaotic tumult of a raging sea or the still waters that nourish the sheep of His pasture. Mem can be a harbinger of confusion and death brought about by a tsunami or it can be a picture of the waters that spring from Messiah and produce a spring of living water in our soul. Mem can mean liquid refreshment or it can mean massive flood waters of doom that bring despair and death. Mem is one of the Hebrew letters that has multiple meanings depending upon your relationship with the Son of God.

PICTOGRAPHIC MEANING OF ELOHIM – A SUMMARY

The last two Hebrew letters in the name of Elohim suggest a further deed to be accomplished besides the work that resulted in the creation of the Earth. A redemptive work is also being forecast. It is a mighty work that comes forth from Elohim. Just as the creation of the physical world was accomplished by the Son of God who spoke the plans of His Father into existence with the aide of the Holy Spirit, God the Father has planned a work of redemption in order to include Man into His heavenly family. It is a plan accomplished by His only begotten Son and revealed by God the Holy Spirit. The Triune God accomplishes the redemption of Man. The first hint of this plan is revealed in the first verse in the ancient prophetic text of Holy Scripture. The creative works of

God have resulted in a blue planet whose waters sustain the life of all its inhabitants. This is a picture of the waters of life that can only be found in Yeshua Ha-Mashiach. He is the Creator who has snatched His fallen children from the death grip of chaos and confusion and given them the life-giving waters that results in new birth, deliverance and salvation.

THE NUMERIC MEANING IN ELOHIM

I would like to remind you that the 22 letters in the Hebrew aleph-beyt are also numbers. For example, the letter aleph is the pictogram of an ox and has the meaning of the strong leader. Aleph is also the number one.

GOD THE FATHER

The first number in the name of Elohim is the Hebrew number aleph. Aleph is represented numerically as the number one. The number one is not only the first number it is also the foundation of all the other numbers. Without the number one you could not have a numeric system.

The number one is the only number that cannot be divided. It needs no other numbers to be complete. The number one is the most important number in the Hebrew aleph-beyt and is unquestionably the number that represents God the Father.

THE BLOOD OF THE LAMB

The second number in the name of Elohim is the Hebrew number lamed. Lamed is represented numerically by the "value" number 30.

The number 30 has a meaning based on how it is used in the Scriptures that corresponds to the blood sacrifices in the Old Testament sacrificial system. In the New Testament it is the number

NUMERIC MEANING OF THE WORD "ELOHIM"

1	א	**Aleph:** Deity, unity, sufficiency, independence, the first, God the Father
30	ל	**Lamed:** Divine deliverance and salvation, the blood of Christ the Lamb of God (3x10), a high degree of the perfection of a divine order as marking the right moment
5	ה	**Hey:** Grace (favor), God's goodness, Pentateuch (first five books of teaching), divine strength, fifth
10	י	**Yood:** Ordinal perfection, perfection of divine order, completeness of order, testimony, law and responsibility
40	מ	**Mem:** Trials, probation, testing, chastisement but no judgment, 5x8 – action of grace revival, 4x10 – renewal or extended rule or dominion

that represents divine deliverance and salvation. The number 30 represents the blood of the Lamb of God.

GRACE

The third number in the name of Elohim is the Hebrew number hey. Hey is represented numerically by the "value" number five. The number five has a meaning based on how it is used in Scripture that corresponds to the idea of unmerited favor or grace.

ORDINAL PERFECTION

The fourth number in the name of Elohim is the Hebrew number yood. Yood is represented numerically by the "value" number 10. The number 10 has a meaning based on how it is used in Scripture that corresponds to the concept of Ordinal Perfection.

Ten is one of four "Perfect" numbers and represents an ordered sequence of events that will take place in order to accomplish a divine purpose.

TRIALS AND PROBATION

The fifth number in the name of Elohim is the Hebrew number mem. Mem is represented numerically by the "value" number 40. The number 40 has a meaning based on how it is used in Scripture that corresponds to the idea of a probationary period of testing.

WHAT THE NUMBERS SAY

God (1) will bring about governmental perfection (10) based on a sequence of events that He has ordained. His divine purposes will be accomplished by the blood sacrifice (30) of the spotless Lamb of God.

God (1) will graciously bring this about at exactly the right time (10).

God (1) will judge and destroy Satan and all those who have rejected the gracious redemptive work (30) of Yeshua Ha-Mashciah. He will test (40) and graciously discipline His own children in order to bring about repentance, revival and renewal.

Elohim

Pictographic translation

Complete reference table, pages 16-17

| Creating Springs of Living Water | A Mighty Deed | Holy Spirit Who Reveals | The Son Who Speaks with Authority | God the Father |

God the Father   The Son Who Speaks with Authority   Holy Spirit Who Reveals A Mighty Deed   Creating Spring os Living Water

Numeric translation

Complete reference table, pages 18-21

God the Father will bring about deliverance through His Annointed One and by His grace bring about a divinely ordained plan, testing Man to show his weakness, and then reviving and renewing Man by His grace.

The Ancient Mystery in 3d Revealed As the Scriptures Unfolded in Time

God the Father, God the Son and God the Holy Spirit participated in the creation of the heavens and the Earth. In the same way the Triune God will test Man to show him his Weakness. After this He will bring about Deliverance and Salvation. God the Father graciously Ordains Man's Renewal. God the Son provides the means in Himself for the Salvation His Father has Ordained. God the Holy Spirit reveals the plans of the Father administered by the Son in order that Man might believe in the Son and be saved.

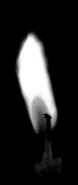  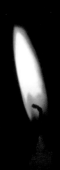

Chapter 5 ~ THE MYSTERY OF THE ALEPH & TAV

א. בראשית ברא אלהים את השמים ואת הארץ

את

tav   aleph

What's in This Word?

Two letters, untranslated, and a signal from God, endlessly repeated

WHAT you are about to read next is, in my opinion, one of the most stunning and provocative revelations in all of Holy Scripture.

If you do not get anything else out of this book I pray you will read and re-read this portion until it sears your heart and fills your soul with wonder and praise.

If you do not recognize Yeshua Ha-Mashiach as the Son of God and Savior of fallen Mankind,

then this is for you. Have you ever wondered at the strange ways God uses to display His glory and majesty?

Much of it is grand and, by using aids like telescopes, our puny view of it becomes even more grand.

His creation is full of His glory and it speaks volumes about the Creator, day and night.

The heavens declare it and so does the Earth. His signature upon His creation is so ubiquitous that there is no excuse for not acknowledging His creative majesty and eternal glory.

We all must recognize and are expected to understand that God has shouted His glory across the Cosmos. Few understand that there is another voice that whispers everlasting truth to all who have ears to hear.

This voice does not seem at first to have any special majestic qualities, but hidden in this whisper, God discloses the humble pathway that leads to eternal life and salvation.

God uses small things – as Man measures smallness – to accomplish great and mighty acts that put His majesty on display.

Five thousand are fed with a lunch designed to feed a child. A child's portion is multiplied by the hand of God to meet the material needs of a multitude.

Look at the Hebrew to English translation on the previous pages and see if you can discover anything unusual. Do you see it?

ALEPH AND TAV

Embedded in the Hebrew text of the Old Testament is a little two-letter "word" that has not been translated and is absent from all current English translations of the Old Testament.

These two letters were given to Moses by the LORD (YHVH) along with all the other Hebrew letters that comprise the first five books of the Torah and the rest of the Hebrew Scriptures.

In other words, so there is no confusion, the aleph and tav that go untranslated in the Hebrew Scriptures were not added. They are part of the original disclosure from God to Man.

If you ask about this anomaly you are told that the aleph and tav (ath) are present as an object marker.

> For example, in Genesis 1:1 we see it for the first time suspended between the word "God" as Creator, and the word "Heaven." It shows up a second time between "Heaven" and "Earth" which, I suppose, is the object being created.

The problem with this explanation is that, if true, it is applied with a degree of randomness that requires further explanations, which I have not discovered.

In other words, the explanation for the anomaly only makes it more mysterious.

What does this mean? Is it an unsolved mystery? Or perhaps this odd pair of letters is a relic of some arcane artifact of the ancient Hebrew language, languishing without any real meaning or purpose.

Perhaps it is a signpost – a marker that is meant to stop the reader and cause him to reflect upon something wondrous, and yes, even mysterious. A hidden treasure perhaps? Or is it just background static – noise without content?

A LOCK AND KEY?

Or maybe it is a lock placed in plain sight to be opened with a key that is yet to be discovered.

If that is the case – and it is a mystery to be unlocked – then may we not expect to find the key somewhere in Scripture? But before we begin our treasure hunt, let's investigate the meaning of the two Hebrew letters aleph and tav.

Aleph is the *first* letter of the Hebrew aleph-beyt. As we have discussed, the Hebrew language – unique to all the other languages in the world – has three layers of revelation.

    The first is the conventional usage as script.
    The second is pictographic.
    The third is numeric.

When harmonized, these three layers are designed by God to reveal and communicate truth. We explored this puzzle in the first chapter of this book. Some of this may start to become familiar.

Aleph

Aleph has stored within it the concepts of divine,

first, and strong leader. Keep in mind we will explore this in depth later in the book.

Tav

Tav is the twenty-second and *final* letter of the Hebrew aleph-beyt.

The meaning of tav is last, covenant, and sign. It is pictured as a cross.

When you put the aleph and tav together it can convey the combined meaning of any or all of the following:

1. The First and Last
2. The Beginning and the End
3. Divine Covenant
4. Divine Sign
5. The entirety of all 22 letters in the Hebrew aleph-beyt is contained between aleph and tav (we might say from A to Z). It can therefore be understood to mean that all the words that proceed from that catalog of letters are the Word.

Let's see if any of these "keys" will unlock the mystery of the aleph and tav as it appears for the first time in the first verse of Genesis.

One of the prominent meanings of aleph and tav is "the first and the last" and "the beginning and the end."

And did you notice where we first find it discreetly placed for us to discover?

The aleph and tav is found in the *first verse* of the *first book* of the Bible, clearly marking the beginning of creation, jetting up for the first time like a flare between God and the heavens.

אֱלֹהִים בָּרָא בְּרֵאשִׁית .א
הָאָרֶץ וְאֵת הַשָּׁמַיִם אֵת

ALEPH AND TAV AND VAV

Notice that the second time aleph tav shows up, it is inserted between Heaven and Earth connected by the Hebrew letter "vav."

ו

Vav

The mystery of the aleph and tav is connected to the meaning of vav in so many ways that in order to fully understand its significance we need to take a few paragraphs to explore the mystery of the sixth letter in the Hebrew aleph-beyt – vav.

Follow along as we pick up important clues about one of the greatest mysteries ever revealed to fallen Mankind! What is the pictogram associated with the letter vav, the sixth letter in the Hebrew aleph-beyt?

The pictogram for vav is an iron nail or wooden peg. (The pictogram of the iron nail is even preserved in the modern Hebrew rendition of the letters of the aleph-beyt). This is what it looks like in English with the Hebrew inserted for emphasis.

Genesis 1:1:
In the beginning God created /*aleph tav*/ the heaven /*vav aleph tav*/ and the earth.

The text at the top of the page shows what it looks like in the original Hebrew. Note that the translation from Hebrew to English is written for your convenience from left to right The individual Hebrew words are written from right to left.

Notice that in the original Hebrew the word "created" appears before the word "God." So when we say that the first aleph and tav insert themselves untranslated between God and Heaven and then again between Heaven and Earth, we are being literal. Now, don't become discouraged if you are not putting this all together. We are just collecting the puzzle pieces. They will be assembled at the end of this chapter. Considering the Hebrew rendering of Genesis 1:1 and applying simple logic we can conclude the following:

> If the aleph and tav are found untranslated, emptied of meaning, is it waiting to be filled with contextual relevancy? If it is, then where might we expect to find the key to this mystery?

If aleph and tav are placeholders for the concept of *beginning and end*, and *first and last*, and if we find the aleph and tav's first occurrence in the first verse in Scripture, then perhaps we will find the answer placed like a bookend in the *last* book of the Bible.

ALPHA AND OMEGA

Let's explore the final book of the Bible and see if we can find anything that might provide the key to unlocking the mystery of the aleph and tav.

As we explore the last chapter of the last book of the Bible we find these amazing words. Is this the key that unlocks the mystery of the aleph and tav? Perhaps! Remember the New Testament is written in Greek, not Hebrew. In the book of Revelation 22:13 Yeshua Ha-Mashiach declares:

> "I am Alpha and Omega, the beginning and the end, the first and the last."

If this is true it should be confirmed by at least two other sources. It is not surprising that we find three more sources that identify the Alpha and the Omega as Yeshua (Jesus). Clearly Yeshua Ha-Mashiach is identifying Himself as the Alpha and Omega – the beginning and the end, the aleph and tav.

> Alpha and omega and aleph and tav are expressions of exactly the same revelation in two languages. Hebrew and Greek both declare exactly the same thing. To be clear – aleph tav and alpha omega are precisely equivalent, or as we might say, exactly the same.

For many this revelation, as it has unfolded to this point in the book, would be sufficient proof that the untranslated aleph and tav is another name for Yeshua Ha-Mashiach. *But there is more, much more!*

As if to secure the point for all those who look with faith upon this revelation, the Lord has arranged for us to view another mystery. With the eyes of our faith now wide open and filled with wonder and amazement, let's explore the second aleph and tav found in Scripture. To do that, we need to continue to explore more deeply the meaning of the Hebrew letter vav.

PUZZLE PIECE ONE: VAV

The sixth letter of the Hebrew aleph-beyt is vav. This letter is interesting as it can mean, "to se-cure" or it can mean the word "and."

But in order to fully understand how this letter operates in Hebrew you need to understand that it can be used as a letter that directly connects with other words and fastens concepts together. The picture for this letter is an iron nail or a wooden peg. When the letter vav comes in contact with another word it can mean that the two words are to be nailed together, or secured to each other.

Let us look again at the first verse of the first book of the Hebrew Bible. In Genesis 1:1 we read the following in English:

> **Genesis 1:1**
> "In the beginning God created the heaven and the earth."

Notice the words "the heaven" and "earth." As we saw earlier in Hebrew, the untranslated aleph and tav is connected to the word "and" that is inserted between Heaven and Earth.

> **Genesis 1:1:**
> In the beginning God created /*aleph tav*/ the heaven /*vav aleph tav*/ and the earth.

Why is aleph and tav connected to the Hebrew letter vav? The mystery further unfolds as you view the pictogram from which the letter tav draws it meaning. The image is of two crossed sticks, a cross.

I doubt at this point that the reader needs me to assemble this disclosure. But for the sake of continuity – and just because it is so glorious to proclaim – let me translate the previously untranslated for my reader.

> The Aleph and the Tav and the Alpha and the Omega are one and the same. It denominates Yeshua Ha-Mashiach.

Yeshua Ha-Mashiach has placed His name between God and Heaven to give Man a prophetic clue as to His majestic identity.

Yeshua Ha-Mashiach has placed His name between Heaven and Earth secured by the image of an iron nail (vav) to give Man a clue as to how He intended to secure Heaven for fallen Mankind. The pictographic meaning of aleph (strong leader, first, God the Father) and tav (sign or covenant pictured as crossed sticks) is obvious to anyone familiar with the historical written testimony of the life, death, and resurrection of Jesus Christ.

In summary – God has made a new covenant with Mankind sealed by the blood of the perfect and spotless Lamb of God, His only Son and our Savior Yeshua Ha-Mashiach. Do you understand the clues?

STRATEGIC PLACEMENT

Now, if the aleph and tav revelation were hidden in just two or three places in God's Word it would be a glorious discovery.

But would it surprise you to learn that this un-translated moniker for the Messiah is one of the most re-occurring and strategic insertions in all of the Old Testament? In order to put this in some context, please consider the following list of the most prominent words in the Scriptures and the number of times they are used.

- Lord (YHVH) – 5,573
- God (Elohim) – 2,687
- King – 1,677
- Sin – 298

So how many times do you think the untranslated aleph and tav shows up? Ten times? Fifty Times? One hundred times?

The answer is stunning. Aleph and tav is inserted into the Scriptures untranslated well over a thou-

sand times! The aleph and tav would easily make the list of the top five words used in the writings of Moses and the Prophets. And it must be added that, having picked and looked at dozens of insertions at random, it was soon discovered that each of these strategic repeated insertions always communicate the same message in one way or another.

> And what is the message? It is simply this – Yeshua Ha-Mashiach is coming and He is the Aleph and the Tav, Alpha and Omega, the Beginning and the End!

It is my belief that the name of Yeshua Ha-Mashiach (Jesus Christ) (aleph and tav) darts upwards like a flaming sword of truth out of the Hebrew Scriptures.

The aleph and tav is not the only divine disclosure regarding Yeshua Ha-Mashiach, but it is certainly the most neglected. Considering the glory and sheer wonder that it is designed to provoke in the mind of fallen Man, don't you think it is time to be widely published? I do.

Could it be that God (YHVH) anticipated the corruption of His revelation and, to ensure the integrity of His message getting through to Mankind intact, encoded and embedded it everywhere in Scripture? Like a hologram, even if you cut a section of it, the essence of the message remains because it is duplicated everywhere without distortion or any missing data.

We could just leave it at that – an amazing discovery that in a very general way makes the point that Yeshua Ha-Mashiach is indeed the sum and substance of the Old Testament.

It is confirmation that Yeshua Ha-Mashiach was the focal point of the earliest promise and prophecies given to our first parents, just as He declared. Or we could find more.

DIVINE ARCHITECTURE

Eve longed for the Son who would be both born and given, and who would bring redemption and restoration from the piercing agony caused by the fall of Man.

Moses, following the precise divine architecture and instructions given by YHVH, built an archetype that in structure, form, and practice prefigured the One who would come to redeem fallen Man. Every temple sacrifice and ceremonial rite ordained upon Mt. Sinai was a foreshadowing of the coming Savior. Moses himself was a type and pattern of the coming Anointed One.

The Feasts of the Lord, outlined in every detail by YHVH were essential prophecies waiting to find their fulfillment in Yeshua Ha-Mashiach.

Enoch first saw Him in the heavens and, according to the book of Enoch, when he inquired as to his identity was told that He was the Son of Man.

Daniel had a vision of Him (the Son of Man) coming in clouds of glory.

Isaiah declared His redemptive mission as the Lamb of God, the suffering Messiah.

Every judge and advocate deliverer of Israel was a shadow figure lighting the darkness in anticipation of the rising of the Son of Righteousness.

He is a prophet like Moses, a king like David and a priest like Melchisadec.

Some stumble at the declaration made by Yeshua Himself that He could be found in the ancient prophetic texts of the Hebrew Old Testament if one would only search.

Based on an overwhelming body of evidence, I am fully persuaded that Yeshua Ha-Mashiach proclaimed the truth when He declared the purpose of the Old Testament.

Jesus said,

John 5:39
"Search the scriptures; for in them ye think ye have eternal life: and they are they which testify of me."

I trust we can agree with St. Peter who described the essence of all who prefigured and prophesied about the coming Savior.

1 Peter 1:11
Searching what, or what manner of time the Spirit of Christ which was in them did signify, when it testified beforehand the sufferings of Christ, and the glory that should follow.

This book is written for two types of people. It is written for those who find it a lavish delight to discover ever more evidence and examples of Yeshua's ubiquitous presence in the ancient prophetic texts.

But this book is also written for those who find it hard to discover Yeshua in the Hebrew Scriptures. Perhaps because His name is not yet visible to them.

For those who love to see His presence in Scripture and for those who have not yet seen it I submit the following further proofs that the aleph and tav is a divinely placed moniker for Yeshua Ha-Mashiach.

I will also show evidence that, in the placement of the two letters aleph and tav, the unfolding mystery of God's plan to redeem Man is revealed in ways that cannot be ignored or dismissed.

א. בראשית ברא אלהים

את השמים ואת הארץ

THE NUMBERS

The first thing I want you to notice is the strategic placement of the first aleph and tav immediately after the Hebrew word Elohim (God).

If you ask why this placement is important, I would simply answer it is a clue and a further disclosure regarding the personage of Elohim. We discovered in the first chapter that the translation of the first three letters of Elohim include an embedded picture of the Trinity – God the Father, God the Son and God the Holy Spirit.

The placement of the aleph and tav is further evidence that the aleph and tav, which is another name for Yeshua Ha-Mashiach, is identifying Himself as the Son of God pictured in the Hebrew word Elohim. Please review the pictograms embedded in the first three letters of the Hebrew word Elohim.

א Aleph: strong leader, first, God the Father – **Ox**

ל Lamed: control, authority, the tongue – **Staff**

ה Hey: reveal, look – **Behold**

The aleph and the tav have been inserted strategically so that the reader might discover the meaning of the aleph and tav and infer its importance because of the prominent placement next to God and between Heaven and Earth. *But wait, there is more.*

Please notice in the graphic above that we have given each letter a number that corresponds with its actual first use in the Hebrew Scriptures. Remember that while the Hebrew shown on these pages is being translated from left to right, the actual Hebrew words are written from right to left.

This explains why the number one appears to be at the end of the Hebrew word b-rashith, when in fact the number one is over the letter beyt, the first letter in the word b-rashith and the first letter in the ancient prophetic Torah.

The next thing I want you to notice are the numbers 15 and 16. These are very special and sacred numbers to the Hebrews. They are considered so sacred that Jews will not write them in the conventional manner so as not to profane what they represent. What do they represent and why are they so important, and what do they have to do with the unfolding revelation regarding the aleph and tav?

The answer is *everything*!

ath – **untranslated in Hebrew**

Pictographic and Numeric translation

Letters below are left to right, transposed for English readers

He is the Beginning and the End

He is the Alpha and the Omega

He is every letter of the Word

He is the entire Word

He is the First and the Last

HE IS YESHUA HA-MASHIACH

Jesus the Christ

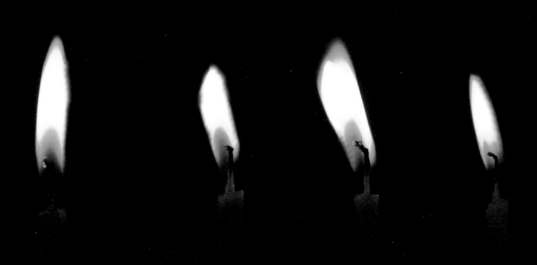

Chapter 6 ~ YAHWEH

Hey   Vav   Hey   Yood

The Mystery of the Name of God

Plus the one candidate who can fulfill the meaning of the code

IN order to understand the profound signifi-cance of the numbers 15 and 16 and what their placement over the aleph and tav mean we need to understand one of the most sacred names in the Hebrew language.

That name cannot be pronounced, as it contains four letters with no vowels. The sacred name connected exclusively with the numbers 15 and 16 is the Hebrew word YHVH – yood hey vav hey.

This is the name of God as revealed in ancient Hebrew Scriptures. The English reader needs to understand that every time he reads "LORD" in the English translation of the Hebrew Old Tes-tament he is reading YHVH in the Hebrew. So, what is the connection between the name YHVH and the numbers 15 and 16? Keep in mind that the Hebrews do not have a separate language for numbers. The Hebrew Numbers are also Hebrew Letters. The number 15 is written in Hebrew as yood hey.

Hey   Yood

The number 16 is written in Hebrew as yood vav.

Vav   Yood

The Hebrews will not write either 15 or 16 in the conventional manner because they contain the root letters in the name of YHVH. We have now seen that the numbers 15 and 16 are considered sacred by the Hebrews because they represent the

PICTOGRAPHIC MEANING OF THE HEBREW WORD YHVH – YAHWEH

י **Yood:** Work, a deed, to make - **Hand**

ה **Hey:** Reveal, look - **Behold**

ו **Vav:** Add, secure - **Wooden Peg Iron Nail**

ה **Hey:** Reveal, look - **Behold**

name of God, YHVH. And what are the 15th and 16th letters as they occur in the first verse of the first chapter in the ancient Hebrew prophetic text? They are the untranslated aleph and tav. The encoded message hidden in plain sight is now simple to decipher. The aleph and tav are identified with the numbers 15 and 16, which represent YHVH.

But, again there is more! If the 15th and 16th as numbers represent YHVH, what does YHVH mean? The Hebrew letters yood hey and vav hey are referred to as the tetragrammaton, or four letter name, which is believed to be pronounced Yahweh (remember, the Hebrew letters above are read backwards). Some English translations of the Old Testament sometimes translate this word as Jehovah.

The word YHVH is considered by the Jews as the holiest name on Earth. Many Jews will never speak it aloud except on Yom Kippur and only by the High Priest. The conventional way the Jews write YHVH is to substitute "G-d." Since Hebrew is written without vowels, we don't know how YHVH was pronounced in the time of Moses. The tetragrammaton YHVH contains no vowels. Early Christian theologians inserted vowels into the tetragrammaton to produce "Yahweh" and "Jehovah." These renderings of YHVH are used by observant Jews, who as we noted, omit the vowel when writing the English word

"G-d." When Jews read the Torah aloud in the synagogue, whenever they come to YHVH, they substitute "Adonai" which means "Lord."

Most Hebrew language scholars believe that when God revealed Himself to Moses, "I am that I am," he was giving the translation of the word "Yahweh" – literally, "I am that I am" (account found in Exodus 3:14.)

Is God saying, "My name is the fact that I exist?" Etymologically, the word "Yahweh" is rooted in words that means "to be" or "to create."

The name "Yahweh" is often rendered "Jehovah." The Hebrew alphabet has no vowels. The name YaHWeH, and YeHoWaH (Jehovah) was arrived at by adding vowels.

Yahweh is the spelling of God's name (in the Roman alphabet) accepted by most non-Jewish scholars. Jehovah is a poor pronunciation and is rejected by all Jewish scholars and many Christians scholars.

Among the problems with the name "Jehovah" is the fact that there is no "j" in the Hebrew language, the closest you can get to it is a "y." The letter "j" has a Germanic etymology and was invented as a letter with the hard "j" sound in the 18th century. Even so, Jehovah is a popular rendering of YHVH among many Christians.

10	**Yood:** Ordinal perfection, perfection of divine order, completeness of order, testimony, law and responsibility
5	**Hey:** Grace (favor), God's goodness, Pentateuch (first five books of teaching), divine strength, fifth
6	**Vav:** Man's world, Man without God, weakness of Man
5	**Hey:** Grace, God's favor, divine strength

The most prominent common usage meanings for YHVH include the following:

> To be, to come into being
> He causes to be, or exist
> He is
> He Creates

CLOSING THE CIRCLE

So, now we have the placement of the aleph and tav connected with the numbers 15 and 16, which are considered by the Hebrews to be sacred numbers that represent God. Coincidence? I think not!

We know the numbers 15 and 16 are considered sacred by the Hebrews because they represent the name of God, YHVH. And we now understand that these are the numbers directly connected with the aleph and tav. And after we investigate the pictographic meaning of the Hebrew letters in the word YHVH – the sacred name of God – then have we not closed the circle on the meaning of the aleph and tav? To whom else would we look?

Behold the Hand - Behold the Nail?

I know of but one candidate who fills in the hidden code with perfection. Let me introduce you to Yeshua Ha-Mashiach! He is the mystery behind the meaning of the numbers 15 and16, the aleph and tav, and the name of YHVH. Let me introduce you to Yeshua Ha-Mashiach! But, there is more!

The numbers 15 and 16 also have a biblical numeric meaning. Besides being revered by the Jews as a number that represents God (10+5), the number 15 also is the number of divine perfection (3) multiplied by grace (5). In other words, the divine perfection of grace. It also means a rest that is brought about by the energy of divine grace and associated with perfect timing or a perfect time.

Resurrection (8) plus spiritual perfection (7) is a special mark of the energy of divine grace issuing in glory. Sixteen is revered by the Jews as a number that represents God. Based on biblical usage the number means love. Based on biblical usage, the combination of the numbers 15 and 16 connected to the aleph and tav can be summarized to mean the following:

As a result of God's love for his fallen creatures, at a specific time ordained in the heavens, the divine energy of grace will result in the resurrection to glory. And who is it who guarantees this outcome and is the first fruits of this resurrection? It is *Yeshua Ha-Mashiach*. But wait! There is more . . .

YHVH – **Yahweh**

Pictographic translation

Complete reference table, pages 16-17

Behold the nail. Behold the hand.

Behold the hand. Behold the nail.

Numeric translation

Complete reference table, pages 18-21

God divinely orders a sequence of events in order
that He might demonstrate grace to Mankind.

The Ancient Mystery in 3d Revealed
As the Scriptures Unfolded in Time

God has revealed His Name to Man so that he might look up and
behold! Twice in the name of YHVH we are commanded to behold
by the authority of the Name that is above every name. Look, look
He pleads! Behold the heartbeat of God! He longs for you to Live by
only looking! Looking in faith and beholding the nail-pierced hands
of Yeshua Ha-Mashiach.

Jesus the Christ

Chapter 7– THE MYSTERY OF THE ALEPH & TAV, PART 2

14 13 12　11　10　　9　8　7　　6　5　4　　3　2　1

א. בראשית ברא אלהים

את השמים ואת הארץ

28　27　26　25　　**24　23** 22　　21 20 19　18　17　　**16 15**

The Death of the Aleph & Tav

And the coming perfection of government

LET'S examine the second occurrence of the Aleph and Tav. If you look at the Aleph and Tav as displayed above you will see that it has the number 23 above the Aleph and the number 24 above the Tav.

As a reminder this number represents the letter count from the first letter in Genesis 1:1 and going forward.

So Aleph is the twenty third letter in the Scrip-tures starting with Genesis 1:1 and Tav is the twenty fourth letter in Scripture starting with Genesis 1:1.

We learned the meaning of the numbers 15 and 16 as associated with the Aleph and the Tav in Chapter 6. Those numbers as you will recall were directly connected to the name of God, YHVH.

Now let's begin by taking a look at the numbers 23 and 24 and see what they might mean

THE NUMBER 23
AND DEATH

The number 23 stands over the Aleph. In Romans 1:28-32 God lists 23 things that, once committed, are worthy of death.

One of the prominent meanings of the number 10 is the *law*. The number that describes the depraved and rebellious heart of man is the number 13. In other words, sin. The number 13 plus 10 equals 23.

> **Romans 7:9** (numbers inserted):
> "I was alive without the law (10) once: when the commandment (law) came, sin (13) revived, and I died (23).

> **1 Corinthians 15:56** says it as follows:
> "The sting of death (23) *is* sin; and the strength of sin (13) *is* the law (10).

THE NUMBER 24
AND GOVERNMENT

The number 24 has two meanings and both are relevant to tav. The first meaning is the concentrated perfection of government.

Remember that 12 is one of four perfect numbers and stands for governmental perfection. The number twenty four also has the biblical meaning associated with the priesthood.

(I highly recommend that you avail yourself of the opportunity to purchase both the "Number in Scripture" book by E. W. Bullinger and "Biblical Mathematics" by Dr. Ed F. Vallowe. Between these two resources you can find more than 500 pages of detailed authoritative studies of the meaning of numbers in Scripture. Unfortunately, it is not within the scope of this text to provide all the references that we are summarizing.)

DEATH, PRIESTHOOD AND
THE NUMBER 1,000

Based on biblical usage, the number 23 forecasts the death of the aleph and tav. And no ordinary death is being forecast. It is a death that is a direct result of the penalty for sin.

And notice that the death penalty hangs above the aleph. Aleph is the number for God. The death of God the Son.

Based on biblical usage, the number 24 forecasts that the aleph and tav would be connected with both the priesthood and the concentrated perfection of government.

That brings another number to mind, the number 1,000. That is the number of years that Messiah will rule and reign on planet Earth.

Until that glorious event unfolds, Yeshua is at the right hand of the Father making intercession for those who have put their faith and trust in him.

In other words Yeshua Ha-Mashiach is our High Priest in Heaven and our soon coming King.

HAVE WE SOLVED THE MYSTERY
OF THE ALEPH AND TAV?

A summary of the clues:

1. Jesus Christ has identified Himself as the first and the last, the beginning and the end, the alpha and the omega.

The alpha and the omega is the Greek translation of the Hebrew aleph and tav They are two expressions in different languages of exactly the same thing.

2. The aleph and tav are placed between God and

Heaven and Heaven and Earth. This is a prophetic clue as to His majestic identity.

3. The picture of an iron nail (vav) next to the aleph and tav and securing Heaven and Earth is a prophetic clue as to how He intended to secure Heaven for fallen Mankind.

4. The pictorial meaning of aleph (strong leader, first, God the Father) and tav (sign, covenant pictured as crossed sticks) is obvious to anyone familiar with the historical written testimony of the life, death and resurrection of Jesus Christ.

5. The aleph and the tav have been inserted strategically so that the reader might discover the meaning of the aleph and tav, inferring its importance because of its prominent placement next to God and between Heaven and Earth.

6. The numbers 15 and16 are considered sacred by the Hebrews because they represent the name of God, YHVH.

The aleph and the tav are the 15th and 16th letters in the first verse of the first chapter in the ancient Hebrew prophetic text.

The encoded message hidden in plain sight is now simple to decipher. The aleph and tav are identified with the numbers 15 and 16, which represent YHVH.

7. YHVH is directly connected with the aleph and tav.

8. The pictographic meaning of the Hebrew letters in the word YHVH is as follows:

Behold the hand. Behold the nail.

9. Based on biblical usage, the combination of the numbers 15 and 16 connected to the aleph and tav have the meaning of the divine energy of grace that will result in the resurrection to glory.

10. Based on biblical usage, the number 23 forecasts the death of the Aleph and Tav. And no ordinary death is being forecast, it is a death that is a direct result of the penalty for sin. And notice that the death penalty hangs above the aleph. Aleph is the number for God. The death of God the Son.

11. Based on biblical usage, the number 24 forecasts that the Aleph and Tav would be connected with both the priesthood and the concentrated perfection of government.

This is a forecast of both the future millennial (1,000 years) reign of Messiah on Earth and the fact that Messiah is currently making intercession for all those who put their faith and trust in Him. He is our heavenly high priest and our soon coming King.

CONCLUSIONS

Have *you* solved the mystery of the aleph and tav? For many of you the answer is a resounding yes!

But for some the presence of Yeshua Ha-Mashiach is still shrouded in a cloud of confusion.

> If that is your condition, then let me give you an encouraging word. The problem is not the absence of Yeshua's presence in the ancient texts. The problem is that you have not the vision to see it. Your mind has been darkened and you need to humbly seek the light.

If Yeshua was indeed absent from the ancient Hebrew Scriptures, then no amount of conjuring or manipulation could place Him there. All attempts would fail the most elementary disciplines of logic and reason.

However, if the problem is our spiritual eyesight, then perhaps a remedy may be found and we may indeed be privileged to gaze upon our Lord and Savior.

As we stated earlier, I rely upon the words of Yeshua when He stated that He was declared everywhere in Scripture.

There are hundreds, if not thousands, of well researched and well written books that disclose the Messiah in hundreds of prophetic Scriptures, leaving the honest searcher with solid evidence that not only is Yeshua the Messiah, but that He forecast His own life and ministry in ways that are unmistakable and indisputable.

Anyone who tells you otherwise is either spiritually blind, has not researched the matter, or is only promulgating someone else's uninformed ignorance.

The Messiah has given enough evidence of His existence and purpose in ministry to satisfy the most rigorous judicial inquiry, and if you choose to ignore the evidence then the burden of proof lies with you, not with Yeshua.

My challenge to anyone in this state of mind is to search, investigate, discover, and pray for enlightenment.

Your eternal destiny hangs in the balance. Do not rest, my friend, until you have found Him. Once found, cling to Him with all the might He gives you.

In Him and Him alone may be found the treasure of all ages, the purpose of all being and the hope of all eternity. Find Him! He promises that if you seek Him with all your heart you will find Him.

Would it surprise you to know that the coming of the Messiah and His fulfillment to the letter of His prearranged agenda is the most documented fact in all of history?

There is more evidence for the existence of the Messiah, His miracle ministry, His death on a cross, and His resurrection from the grave than there is for the existence of Plato or Aristotle.

It is the purpose of this inquiry to declare the ubiquitous presence of Yeshua Ha-Mashiach in the ancient Hebrew text. It is also the purpose of this inquiry to substantiate the claim by exploring a path that has been hitherto hidden or ignored.

I am working under the presupposition that the placement of the aleph and tav is both strategic and intentionally designed to mark majestic and magisterial treasure that adorns Yeshua.

I am further persuaded that an inquiry into this matter will enlighten our minds and souls with the certainty of the presence of Yeshua in the text.

I am very limited in what I can disclose. The true revelation must come from the Holy Spirit.

Has enough evidence been presented so that you might bend the knee, humble yourself and simply pray that God would reveal Himself to you?

Matthew 11:25,26
At that time Jesus answered and said, I thank thee, O Father, Lord of heaven and earth, because thou hast hid these things from the wise and prudent, and hast revealed them unto babes. Even so, Father: For so it seemed good in thy sight.

ath – **untranslated in Hebrew**

Pictographic and Numeric translation

I am Alpha and Omega,

the beginning and the end,

the first and the last.

Signed *Jesus the Christ*

Recorded by the Apostle John

in the book of Revelation 22:13

Chapter 8 – THE HEAVENS

A Divine Signature

And your privilege to behold it

THE heavens are the visual canopy that has inspired Man's imagination since the dawn of time. Look up on a clear night and you can lose yourself in the sheer wonder and vastness of the starry hosts of Heaven.

There is nothing remotely like it on Earth and it can only be seen by bending the neck and gazing upward. It is over our heads, beyond our reach and it constantly beckons us to consider matters wonderful and perplexing. Is it really a surprise that the first letter in the Hebrew word for the heavens is the letter hey?

The original pictographic letter in the ancient Hebrew was a stick man with his arms lifted up to the heavens. Hey means *to look up or behold*. The meaning of this is designed to be obvious. There is something important and noteworthy that we are to observe. Something is going to be revealed. The question is what?

Job 35:5
Look unto the heavens, and see; and behold the clouds which are higher than thou.

The first time the letter hey appears in the ancient Scriptures is in Genesis 1:1. Hey is the twelfth letter revealed in Scripture and is connected to the third word in Scripture.

The numbers 12 and 3 are both "perfect" numbers. The number 12 is the number of *governmental perfection.*

The number three is the number of *divine perfection.* Combine them and you have the picture of a divinely ordered system of governance that is perfect in its design and its administration. The heavens are physical evidence of this majestic reality. So what is the third word in the Hebrew Scriptures? If you guessed Elohim you are right. In the middle of the Hebrew word for God is the letter hey.

Why is this important? The answer is amazing. In Hebrew the letter in the middle of a word has special significance. It is a letter that gives you a clue as to the essence of the entire word.

Hebrew spelling of verse

א. בראשית ברא אלהים
את השמים ואת הארץ

Hebrew pronunciation of verse

Be•re•shéet ba•ra Elohím | et ha•sha•má•yim | ve•et ha•á•retz

English translation of verse

(Left to right) English

1. In the Beginning God created the heaven and earth

(Right to left) Hebrew

א. בראשית ברא אלהים
את השמים ואת הארץ

e shmim – *pronounced et ha.sha.má•yim*

Mem	Yood	Mem	Sheen	Hey
40	10	40	300	5

NUMERIC MEANINGS OF E - SHMIM

5	ה	**Hey:** Grace (favor), God's goodness, Pentateuch (first five books of teaching), divine strength, fifth
300	ש	**Sheen:** Divine spiritual order brought about by a divine act of restoration. Restoration which can only follow a gracious perfect blood sacrifice which puts an end to Man's sin and thus restores Man to the fellowship and relationship with God. Victory over God's enemies and over sin brought about by supernatural means.
40	מ	**Mem:** Trials, probation, testing, chastisement but no judgment, 5x8 – action of grace revival, 4x10 – renewal or extended rule or dominion
10	י	**Yood:** Ordinal perfection, perfection of divine order, completeness of order, testimony, law and responsibility
40	ם	**Mem:** Trials, probation, testing, chastisement but no judgment, 5x8 – action of grace revival, 4x10 – renewal or extended rule or dominion

The Hebrew letter hey showing up in the middle of the name of God should come as a great comfort to us. Hey, as we have already learned, is the letter that means behold or look. Hey is also the one Hebrew letter most often connected to God the Holy Spirit. He is the ultimate revelator.

HEY AND THE NUMBER FIVE

Hey, the first letter in the Hebrew word "the heavens," is also the fifth letter in the Hebrew aleph-beyt and it signifies the *number five*. Five is the number for *grace*.

It is very reassuring to know that the God who invites us to look and behold is the same God who graciously stands ready to enlighten us as to what it is He would have us behold.

We are not left to wander in the dark, but rather are offered a guided tour designed to reshape our fallen minds and illuminate our understanding. This privilege is not earned and cannot be purchased. It is all of grace and grace alone.

When your cry of the heart is "leave me alone" you may get your wish.

But the cry of your heart is "Lord reveal yourself to me" you can expect the lamp to be lit so that you might take the first steps along the path God has built for those who wish to take a journey that has its conclusion in Him. And when you find yourself in Him you will be overcome with the majesty of God's grace.

The letter hey communicates His desire for you to behold a revelation. What is it that God wants to reveal?

Before we answer that question let's consider why you are given the privilege to behold and consider the majesty of God in the first place. What is the impulse that makes this revelation possible? It is grace!

75

Psalm 19:1
The **heavens** declare the glory of God; and the firmament sheweth his handiwork.

The question still remains: How are we to understand what we are looking upon as we gaze at the heavens? The answer is given in the second Hebrew letter in the word "the heavens."

Sheen

SHEEN AND THE NAME OF GOD

The Hebrew letter sheen is one of the most mysterious and important letters in the Hebrew aleph-beyt. There are three basic concepts contained in the letter sheen. These three concepts are all unique and yet connected in ways you are about to discover. The pictograph for the letter sheen is teeth. The three pictogram concepts embedded in the Hebrew letter sheen are as follows:

1. God's name
2. To consume or destroy
3. To press against

Which meaning would you pick? Before you decide, let's examine all three picture meanings that are connected with the Hebrew letter Sheen, starting with God's Name.

GOD'S NAME - A DIVINE SIGNATURE

Sheen is the one letter that is connected with the name of God. Would it surprise you that God has written His name on the Earth? In the ancient prophetic text of Deuteronomy we read the following:

Deuteronomy 12:11
Then to the place the Lord your God will choose as a dwelling for his name - there you are to bring everything I command you: your burnt offerings and sacrifices, your tithes and special gifts, and all the choice possessions you have vowed to the Lord.

Where is this place that God has inscribed His name? The answer is Jerusalem. Jerusalem was the place where the Hebrew's were to come and offer their sacrifices.
Jerusalem is where the temple was eventually built.

Before we proceed, please read the following verses in order to be fully persuaded that God actually said that He would put His name in Jerusalem. Are we to understand this literally? You decide.

1 Kings 11:36
And unto his son will I give one tribe, that David my servant may have a light alway before me in Jerusalem, the city which I have chosen me to put my name there.

2 Kings 21:4
And he built altars in the house of the LORD, of which the LORD said, In Jerusalem will I put my name.

2 Kings 21:7
And he set a graven image of the grove that he had made in the house, of which the LORD said to David, and to Solomon his son, In this house, and in Jerusalem, which I have chosen out of all tribes of Israel, will I put my name forever:

2 Chronicles 6:6
But I have chosen Jerusalem, that my name might be there;

2 Chronicles 33:4
Also he built altars in the house of the LORD, whereof the LORD had said, In Jerusalem shall my name be forever.

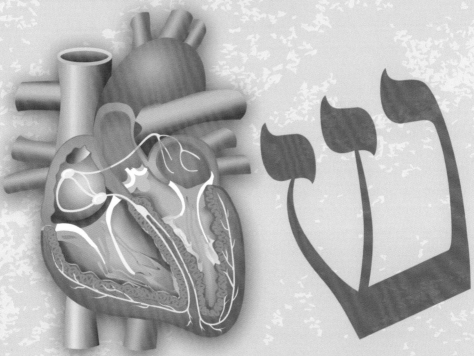

Notice the ancient map of Jerusalem on th previous page. Consider that the three valleys that come together at the base of Mount Moriah etch into stone the Hebrew letter sheen, the name of God. Notice the Kidron Valley on the right, the Central Valley in the middle, and the Hinom Valley on the left – the three fingers that hide a revelation and reveal the title holder's name. Is this the place where God literally chose to write His name?

GOD'S NAME - EL SHADDAI

Abraham, Isaac and Jacob all knew God as El Shaddai, which means Almighty God. It was El Shaddai who told Abraham to look up at the stars and count them, with the promise that God would make his descendants as plentiful as the starry hosts. The concept of almighty is embedded in the Hebrew letter sheen. It is only important that you understand that the first letter of "Shaddai" is the letter sheen and it is meant to emphasize God's awesome power and might.

GOD'S NAME - SHEEN AND THE TRINITY

If you hold your fingers up as if to show someone the number three, you have pictured sheen. Don't you think that is interesting? Is this a picture of the Trinity? You decide.

GOD'S NAME - SHEEN AND THE HUMAN HEART

There is one other place God may have chosen to write His name: Consider the cross section of the human heart on the previous page.

CONSUME OR DESTROY – AND THE LETTER SHEEN

The second possible meaning of the letter sheen is to consume or to destroy. At first this seems like an odd puzzle piece that does not fit the grand idea of "the heavens." But let's look into it a little deeper before we discard this meaning.

There is no question that God has directed us to look upward and consider the heavens as a display of His amazing creative power and might. What an awesome calling card, unlike anything else imaginable. Through the centuries men have looked upward and, instead of seeing the heavens as the handiwork of the Creator, have vainly imagined that the heavens themselves are to be worshipped.

God gives a warning to those who would corrupt the message of creation and vainly imagine things instead of meditating upon the One who created all things.

Deuteronomy 4:19
And lest thou lift up thine eyes unto heaven, and when thou seest the sun, and the moon, and the stars, even all the host of heaven, shouldest be driven to worship them, and serve them, which the Lord thy God hath divided unto all nations under the whole heaven

We are not left to wonder if this admonition was heeded. It was not.

2 Kings 17:16
And they left all the commandments of the Lord their God, and made them molten images, even two calves, and made a grove, and worshipped all the host of heaven, and served Baal

What happens when man willingly ignores God's glory as revealed in the heavens? Read what the apostle Paul declares regarding the matter.

Romans 1:19-20
Because that which may be known of God is

PICTOGRAPHIC MEANINGS OF E - SHMIM

Hey: Reveal, look - **Behold**

Sheen: To consume, to destroy, God's name - **Teeth**

Mem: Liquid, massive, chaos - **Water**

Yood: Work, a deed, to make - **Hand**

Mem: Liquid, massive, chaos - **Water**

---

manifest in them; for God hath shewed it unto them. For the invisible things of him from the creation of the world are clearly seen, being understood by the things that are made, even his eternal power and Godhead; so that they are without excuse:

Clearly "the heavens" are chief among the creative works of God. Clearly they have one purpose as it regards Mankind. And what is that purpose? The answer can be found in the verse that continues the thought declared in Romans 1:19-20.

> **Romans 1:21**
> Because that, when they knew God, they glorified him not as God, neither were thankful; but became vain in their imaginations, and their foolish heart was darkened

If we reverse engineer this verse we discover the purpose of the creative works of God as it relates to Mankind. And what is that purpose?

The answer is that men might *glorify* God and be *thankful* for all His mighty works that remind us continually of His creative majesty and sustaining power.

WILL THE HEAVENS BE CONSUMED?

It took Albert Einstein to prove that, left to its own devices, the cosmos would come to an end one day.

Do you know why this is true? Because the universe we view and attempt to understand is in the process of *consuming* itself. It is the ultimate energy consumer. Let me remind you that one of the prominent pictographic meanings of sheen, the first letter in the Hebrew word heaven, is *consume*.

In other words, one of the elementary disclosures regarding the cosmos is that, left to an un-interrupted destiny, one day it is going to begin running out of fuel and simply go into a chilly death spiral.

Our Sun will go from a blazing, giant ball to a shrunken, crispy, white ember called a white dwarf. But have no fear: the universe is not going to die a natural death!

Do you know why the heavens will never run out energy and consume itself? The answer is revealed in the following quotes from the ancient prophetic text.

Isaiah 51:6
Lift up your eyes to the heavens, and look upon the earth beneath: for the heavens shall vanish away like smoke, and the earth shall wax old like a garment, and they that dwell therein shall die in like manner: but my salvation shall be for ever, and my righteousness shall not be abolished

And, as a reminder, the other prominent pictographic meaning of sheen, the first letter in the Hebrew word heaven, is *to destroy*.

The heavens are not going to run out of *energy*, they are going to run out of *time*.

The Creator has fixed the time for the heavens to be rolled up like a scroll, and with a great noise it will melt with a fervent heat and be no more.

Revelation 6:14
And the heaven departed as a scroll when it is rolled together; and every mountain and island were moved out of their places.

2 Peter 3:10
But the day of the Lord will come as a thief in the night; in the which the heavens shall pass away with a great noise, and the elements shall melt with fervent heat, the earth also and the works that are therein shall be burned up.

2 Peter 3:7
But the heavens and the earth, which are now, by the same word are kept in store, reserved unto fire against the Day of Judgment and perdition of ungodly men.

2 Peter 3:12
Looking for and hasting unto the coming of the day of God, wherein the heavens being on fire shall be dissolved, and the elements shall melt with fervent heat?

And then what happens?

Isaiah 65:17
For, behold, I create new heavens and a new earth: and the former shall not be remembered, nor come into mind.

Revelation 21:1
And I saw a new heaven and a new earth: for the first heaven and the first earth were passed away; and there was no more sea.

Matthew 24:35
Heaven and earth shall pass away, but my words shall not pass away

TO PRESS AGAINST – AND THE LETTER SHEEN

The third picture meaning for the letter Sheen is *to press against*.

The idea of pressing can have several meanings. A king may press his ring against the melted wax to seal a document and to inform anyone that looks upon it that they are viewing a royal decree.

Are the heavens, metaphorically speaking, a letter that has been pressed with the royal insignia? Something to consider.

When you press against something it may be for the purpose of securing it or connecting it to something else.

Are we to understand as we view the heavens that we are being pressed to make a connection to something else? What might that something be?

Could it be the humbling revelation that God is God and we are His creatures? Could it be that we are being "pressed" to acknowledge God as the Creator or all things? Or is something else in view?

Could the connection between Man and the heavens be a veiled reference to the Son of God who has secured Heaven for us by ways and means alluded to in shadows and types.

Obviously there is more here than meets the physical eye. Perhaps the number connected with sheen will shed some light on this possible spiritual connection.

SHEEN AND THE NUMBER 300

We have examined some of the possible pictographic meanings of the letter sheen, now let's look at the number represented by the Hebrew letter sheen.

The number 300 is a number about which most Christians have no opinion. In order to understand the significance of this number let's look to Scripture and see how the number is used. The number 300 is not explained in any of the books on biblical numbers. This provided me with the opportunity to discover the meaning for myself. In order to accomplish this I looked up every instance in the Scriptures where the number 300 was used as a stand-alone number. I hope this will give you some confidence in the way the numeric meaning is discerned as we discover how the number is used in Scripture.

300 = Victory over death:
Genesis 5:22
And Enoch walked with God after he begat Methuselah three hundred years, and begat sons and daughters:

300 = Grace:
Genesis 45:22
To all of them he gave each man changes of raiment; but to Benjamin he gave three hundred pieces of silver, and five changes of raiment.

300 = Victory over Enemy:
Judges 7:7
And the Lord said unto Gideon, By the three hundred men that lapped will I save you, and deliver the Midianites into thine hand: and let all the other people go every man unto his place.

300 = Victory over Enemy:
Judges 15:4
And Samson went and caught three hundred foxes, and took firebrands, and turned tail to tail, and put a firebrand in the midst between two tails.

300 = Victory over Enemy:
2 Samuel 23:18
And Abishai, the brother of Joab, the son of Zeruiah, was chief among three. And he lifted up his spear against three hundred, and slew them, and had the name among three.

300 = Victory over Enemy:
1 Chronicles 11:11
And this is the number of the mighty men whom David had; Jashobeam, an Hachmonite, the chief of the captains: he lifted up his spear against three hundred slain by him at one time.

300 = Victory over Enemy:
1 Chronicles 11:20
And Abishai the brother of Joab, he was chief of the three: for lifting up his spear against three hundred, he slew them, and had a name among the three.

300 = Grace and Deliverance
Genesis 6:15
And this is the fashion which thou shalt make it of: The length of the ark shall be three hundred cubits, the breadth of it fifty cubits, and the height of it thirty cubits.

300 = Burial and Resurrection of the Messiah:

John 12:5
Why was not this ointment sold for three hundred pence, and given to the poor?

I found the number 300 used 24 times. The number 24 is the number of *government perfection multiplied.*

Interesting that the first use of the number 300 is in reference to Enoch who did not die. The second reference to the number 300 is in reference to Noah, who by God's grace was saved from the flood.

The last reference is to the anointing of Jesus with ointment in preparation for his death and burial.

It was Jesus himself who prophecied that this act of love and devotion would be a part of the gospel story of His death, burial and resurrection.

There is special importance given to the first and last time a word or number is used. In this particular case the meaning could not be more clear. The number 300 is the number of *new life and resurrection.*

All the other scriptural references, including the ones not listed in this book, refer to a supernatural victory over the enemies of God.

Gideon and his band of 300 are victorious over the enemy supernaturally. Samson is given the ability to perform impossible feats of strength and victory over the enemies by supernatural means. And the final example of the number 300 in the Scriptures is a picture of grace and resurrection.

THE NUMERICAL MEANING

The meaning of the number 300 is clear based on how it is used in Scripture. It clearly means victory over the enemies of God. The number 300 is connected with the grace of God and the Son of God's victory over death and the grave. Three hundred is an awesome number connected with sheen the second letter in the Hebrew word "the heavens!"

MEM YOOD MEM

Instead of dealing with the last three Hebrew letters in the word "the heavens" individually we will look at them as a unit. The reason for this will become obvious.

    Mem: liquid, massive, chaos - Water
    Yood: work, a deed, to make - Hand
    Mem: liquid, massive, chaos - Water

Genesis 1:7-8
And God made the firmament, and divided the waters which were under the firmament from the waters which were above the firmament: and it was so. And God called the firmament Heaven

Obviously the last three Hebrew letters in the word "the heavens" describe perfectly the events described that took place on the second day of creation:

Water – Deed – Water

It is the awesome, creative work of the heavens that God points to as evidence of His power and glory.

There is nothing except His own Son that God directs our attention to more frequently than the heavens. Do you know why?

God himself discloses the answer. The prerequisite to faith is to believe that God *is*. God points man to the heavens as proof positive that He is.

The journey of faith begins with acknowledging that God is the creator of all things. God admonishes us to consider the heavens the work of His hands.

SIGNS IN THE HEAVENS

The heavens declare God's glory. That glory never radiates brighter than it does on an annual basis as it identifies the times that men are to stop and consider the redemptive plan of Yeshua Ha-Mashiach. And how does it do that, you might ask?

The answer has been largely ignored: the signs of the heavens are used to mark Gods appointed times on Earth.

The Seven Feasts of the Lord are marked on His celestial calendar by new moons and full moons.

The Feasts of the Lord are a prophetic rehearsal of the Gospel message from start to finish.

There is an interplay between Heaven and Earth for the purpose of directing Man to consider and rehearse the unfolding redemptive plan of God.

To learn more about the signs in the heavens as appointments that God has with Man for the purpose of unfolding His redemptive plan, I suggest you go on the internet and type - God's Prophetic Calendar – into the search box.

Everyone from the casual observer to the professional astronomer comes to the same conclusion when viewing the heavens.

It does not matter whether you are looking through your own eyes or having your vision magnified by a high-powered telescope. The heavens are massive in their architectural scope and massive in their relationship to everything else we know and experience.

The heavens are massively incomprehensible as a deed or a work, but easily understood as a display. God does not admonish us to look up and try and figure it out.

He does not ask us to behold and doubt. God simply asks us to cast our eyes upward and consider the work of His hands.

That is the revelation. The response should be obvious.

We are invited every evening to reconsider the awesome celestial display and then worship and praise the Creator who made it all.

e-shmim– **the heaven**

Pictographic translation

Complete reference table, pages 16-17

Separating the Waters   God Almighty   Behold

Behold God Almighty Separating the Waters

Numeric translation

Complete reference table, pages 18-21

Grace that brings about divine restoration and salvation
through a period of trials and testing in which God does a mighty deed
that reveals Man's weakness and insufficiency so that God might
graciously bring about revival and renewal.

The Ancient Mystery in 3d Revealed
As the Scriptures Unfolded in Time

Behold God Almighty Who made the heavens. This same God is going to
bring about restoration and salvation. He has ordained a period of trials and
testing in order that Man might fully understand his weakness and
feebleness. This is necessary so that Man might abandon any hope he
might have in himself. Man must humbly wait for the restoration and
salvation that God will bring about at the appointed time. At the set time
Man will see God's grace on display, high and lifted up.

Chapter 9 – AND THE EARTH

Earth is God's Stage

God is unfolding His eternal plan to redeem and reconcile Man, and the setting He has chosen is the Earth

EARTH seen from space is the Blue Planet, sometimes called the Blue Marble. Earth is the third-closest planet to the Sun and the largest of the Solar System's terrestrial planets.

It is the only planet known in the entire Cosmos to accommodate life. God created Earth as a home for millions of species, including the pinnacle of His creation and the only created being we know of who God made with His own hands – Man.

The genealogy of Man began with one man, whom God named Adam, and into whom He breathed the breath of life. Man was made in the image of God and still bears His image.

His original vocation, as God's representative, was to rule Earth and take dominion over all that God had created upon the Earth. This royal vocation was revoked when Man rebelled against God and became separated from his Creator.

Earth is the stage upon which God is unfolding His eternal plan to redeem and reconcile Man. The purpose of Earth is not what you might suppose, and will be revealed in the following pictographic translation of the meaning of the Earth.

THE ORIGIN AND OWNERSHIP OF THE EARTH

Before we explore the topic of the Earth as it is disclosed in the 3-D Scriptures, the preeminent foundational truth is that God wants there to be no mistake about the origin and ownership of Earth.

The Earth is the Lord's! The following Scriptures leave no doubt as to the fundamental understanding we are to have when it comes to the Earth.

Exodus 9:29
And Moses said unto him, As soon as I am gone out of the city, I will spread abroad my hands unto the LORD; and the thunder shall cease, neither shall there be any more hail; that thou mayest know how that the earth is the LORD'S.

Psalm 24:1
The Earth is the LORD'S and the fullness thereof, the world and those who dwell therein.

Hebrew spelling of verse

א. בראשית ברא אלהים
את השמים ואת הארץ

Hebrew pronunciation of verse

Be•re•shéet ba•ra Elohím et ha•sha•má•yim | ve•et ha•á•retz |

English translation of verse

(Left to right) English

1. In the Beginning God created the heaven and earth

(Right to left) Hebrew

א. בראשית ברא אלהים
את השמים ואת הארץ

e artz– *pronounced ve•et ha•á•retz*

ואת הארץ

Tsade	Reysh	Aleph	Hey		Tav	Aleph	Vav
90	200	1	5		400	1	6

Psalm 89:11

The heavens are thine, the earth also is thine: as for the world and the fulness thereof, thou hast founded them.

Jeremiah 10:12

He hath made the earth by his power, he hath established the world by his wisdom, and hath stretched out the heavens by his discretion.

I Corinthians 10:26

For the earth is the Lord's, and the fulness thereof.

Hebrews 1:10

And, Thou, Lord, in the beginning hast laid the foundation of the earth; and the heavens are the works of thine hands:

So the mystery of the Earth is not who owns it, although many in these days of growing rebellion and unbelief are willfully confused about its origin and ownership. The purpose of this study is to disclose the mystery of the Earth and to discover its ultimate and primary purpose.

WHAT IS THE PURPOSE OF THE EARTH?

We are told in the second verse of the first chapter of Genesis that "the Earth was without form, and void." The Hebrew word for void is e-beu, pronounced bohu in English.

The KJV translates this word as void. But this misses the original targeted concept that is being communicated by the Hebrew word e-beu.

The word e-beu means vacant, vacancy or vacated. The common usage meaning is that the Earth was uninhabitable. And, as we learned earlier, God declares that He makes nothing e-beu, or uninhabitable.

So when God arrives on the cosmic scene, He reveals to us that the once habitable and highly organized Earth had become chaotic and uninhabitable.

We have a scant amount of information regarding the events that took place in the third Heaven where God resides. But even with this small amount of information, it takes little imagination to understand that the chaotic condition of Earth was connected with the casting out of Satan and the war that ensued, all predating the re-creation of planet Earth. Clearly there is a history connected with Earth that we are left to consider and ponder. The question before us is as follows: Is Earth the ancient title of our planet? In other words, is there a meaning in the Hebrew word Earth that expresses an idea that predates the re-creation of Earth and the creation of Man?

God makes a clear distinction in His word between the world and the Earth. The world currently is under the management and administration of the prince of darkness, Satan. But we are told that the Earth is the Lord's. I will let you follow this thread on your own, because I am simply making a distinction for the purpose of clarifying the purpose of the Earth and not the world.

Tsade

THE FISH HOOK

There is one letter in the Hebrew word "the Earth" that deserves special attention and clarification, and that is the letter tsade. In the original Hebrew this letter was pictured and understood to be a fish hook.

Obviously this letter can be quite literally connected to a fish. We all understand what it means to be hooked on something. The Hebrew word for

PICTOGRAPHIC MEANINGS OF E - ARTZ

Hey: reveal, look - **Behold**

Aleph: strong leader, the first, God the Father - **Ox**

Reysh: a person, the head the highest - **Head**

Tsade: catch, desire, need – **Fish Hook**

thirst, for example, is tza-ma:

Aleph - Mem - Tsade
thirst

This is the pictogram of being strongly hooked (tsade) on water. The following is a picture of the heart with a hook in it. The Hebrew word ra-tza has the meaning of having a strong affection or wanting something with all your heart. In English we might say "the hearts desire" to express a strong attachment or affection for something.

Hey - Tsade -Reysh
desire

We will look at both the hidden meanings of thirst and desire in another volume. But for now it is only necessary that you understand the general context and pictographic meaning of the Hebrew letter tsade. Now let's move forward with the picture of tsade and see if we can discover its connection to a fish.

THE FISH HOOK AND THE FISH

It is interesting that the 14th letter of the Hebrew aleph-beyt is noon and the underlying pictogram is a fish and the predominant meaning of the letter is life. Keep this clue in mind.

Noon

Is there a mystery in the relationship between the letter pictured as a fish hook and the letter pictured as a fish?

Matthew 4:18-19
And Jesus, walking by the sea of Galilee, saw two brethren, Simon called Peter, and Andrew his brother, casting a net into the sea: for they were fishers.
19 And he saith unto them, 'Follow me, and I will make you fishers of men'.

The first century symbol of the Christians that survives to this day is the emblem or picture of a fish. What does it mean? Christians have been hooked on life, the life that comes from desiring and trusting in the Messiah, the Son of God, the Savior. Embedded in the Hebrew letter tsade is the picture of a fish hook. Implicit in the fish hook is the idea of catching fish. Is it a coincidence that Jesus Christ declared to His followers that they would become fishers of men? And what was the hook that men would desire more than anything else in this world? The answer to that question is found in the next Hebrew letter we need to ex-

plore which is reysh. In the original Hebrew, this letter was pictured as a head and understood to be the head man, chief or prince. We first encountered the Hebrew letter reysh as we explored the amazing prophecy contained in the first word found in the Torah (b-rashith – In Beginning).

b - rashith

It was there we discovered the pictographic prophecy regarding the cross on which the Son (beyt reysh) of God would willingly give His life as a sacrifice for our sins. We noticed that the letter reysh, being the second letter revealed in the ancient prophetic text, numerically signifies that it was the Son of the most high, the Prince of Heaven, Who is in view.

Matthew 27:33-37

And when they were come unto a place called Golgotha, that is to say, a place of a skull,
34 They gave him vinegar to drink mingled with gall: and when he had tasted thereof, he would not drink.
35 And they crucified him, and parted his garments, casting lots: that it might be fulfilled which was spoken by the prophet, They parted my garments among them, and upon my vesture did they cast lots.
36 And sitting down they watched him there;
37 And set up over his head his accusation written, THIS IS JESUS THE KING OF THE JEWS.

The picture revelation contained in the two letters tsade and reysh can be translated as follows: Desire the Son. Add the other two letters, aleph and hey, and you have the following message:

Behold God's Son and Desire Him

Add the common usage meaning of the Hebrew word "the Earth" and you have the expanded message as follows: The purpose of the Earth is to reveal the Creator, the Son of God Whom we are to behold and desire above all!

Psalm 42:1

As a deer pants for flowing streams, so pants my soul for you, O God.

Psalm 2:12

Kiss the Son, lest he be angry, and ye perish from the way, when his wrath is kindled but a little. Blessed are all they that put their trust in him.

John 17:3

And this is life eternal, that they might know thee the only true God, and Jesus Christ, whom thou hast sent.

John 3:36

He that believeth on the Son hath everlasting life: and he that believeth not the Son shall not see life; but the wrath of God abideth on him.

Psalms 10:27

The LORD is my strength and my shield; my heart trusts in him, and he helps me. My heart leaps for joy, and with my song I praise him.

Psalms 28:7

And he answering said, Thou shalt love the Lord thy God with all thy heart, and with all thy soul, and with all thy strength, and with all thy mind; and thy neighbour as thyself.

Joshua 23:11

Take good heed therefore unto yourselves, that ye love the LORD your God.

Psalms 73:25

Whom have I in heaven but thee? And there is none upon earth that I desire beside thee.

THE MYSTERY OF THE TRINITY

The Hebrew word "the Earth" begins with the letter hey (remember that Hebrew is read from right to left). The ancient pictogram of hey is the image of a man holding up both hands in the air as he looks up. The prominent meaning is to reveal or behold.

Hey

The number for hey is the number five. Five is the number signifying grace.

You can't have a revelation or a wonder to behold without a revelator. The Holy Spirit is pictured and numbered in the Hebrew word "the Earth" as the gracious revelator.

The second letter in the Hebrew word "the Earth" is the letter aleph.

Aleph

Aleph is the first letter in the Hebrew aleph-beyt and in the context of this word represents God the Father.

Notice that in the Hebrew word "the Earth," the prince (reysh) is not coming out of the house (beyt) of the father but is coming forth out of the father (aleph).

The third letter in the Hebrew word "the Earth" is the letter reysh.

Reysh is the prince or the head man. In the context of the Hebrew word "the Earth," it signifies the Son of God.

Reysh

As we illustrated in an earlier portion of this book, the Hebrew word for Father (ABBA) is pictured as the Strong Leader (aleph) of the tent or house (beyt).

Abba in Hebrew is spelled aleph beyt. We also illustrated in an earlier portion of this book that the prince or headman (reysh) who comes forth out of the house (beyt) is the son. Bar or son in Hebrew is spelled beyt reysh.

So let's add some nuance to the meaning of the Hebrew word "the Earth," adding the final letter Tsade to emphasize the concept of Desire. Might we not express it as follows:

Tsade

The Spirit of God reveals that the Son of God, the Prince of Heaven, has come forth from God the Father and is **to be desired** above everything else on the Earth.

The mystery continues to unfold as we widen the lens and explore the context in which the mystery of the meaning of the Earth finds itself.

THE ENCODED MESSAGE

The Hebrew word "the Earth" is introduced by "and" (opposite page). In English this slides right past us without sounding the slightest alarm.

But once you understand the mystery of the aleph and tav and the pictographic meaning of the letter vav, a stunning revelation emerges.

א. בראשית ברא אלהים
את השמים ואת האר ץ

Let us take a look at this amazing prophetic mystery hidden between the heavens and Earth.

As we discovered earlier, the mystery of the aleph and tav is solved once you understand that it is the moniker for the Messiah, the watermark of the Creator, the Beginning and the End, the Alpha and the Omega.

And where do we find the aleph and tav, the moniker for the Messiah? Between Heaven and Earth.

The picture here is clearly one of mediation. If we are ever, as fallen Mankind, to inhabit Heaven, it will only be made possible by the person Yeshua Ha-Mashiach, the Aleph and Tav.

But how will this breach between Man and his Creator be healed?

We have just discovered that the pictographic embedded mystery of the Hebrew word "the Earth" is encoded with the message that the purpose of Earth is to reveal the Creator, the revelation working in our very soul a desire to know and worship Him. But why?

What is the hook that so connects us to the Son of God in a way that consumes our thoughts and fills our hearts with a desire for Him, and that overpowers and dims all the vanities and pleasures of this world? What is it?

The answer to this question is hidden in a single

Hebrew letter, the letter vav. It is the vav that secures the aleph and tav to the Earth.

Vav is the sixth letter of the Hebrew aleph-beyt and it is pictured as an iron nail and a wooden peg.

ו

Vav

So let's unravel the mystery and disclose the message contained in the Hebrew words "and the Earth."

The key that connects sinful Man to an unquenchable desire for the Son of God is an iron nail and a wooden peg.

This would have been left an unsolved mystery until the final solution was Himself nailed, hands and feet, to a wooden cross.

The hook pictured in the pictographic mystery of the meaning of the Hebrew word "the Earth" is finally unveiled – the reason for the strong desire to be connected to the Son of God.

John 12:32-33
Jesus said… And I, if I be lifted up from the earth, will draw all men unto me.
33 This he said, signifying what death he should die.

5	ה	**Hey:** Grace
1	א	**Aleph:** Deity, unity, sufficiency, independence, the first, God the Father
200	ר	**Reysh:** Man's Insufficiency, God's Sufficiency
90	צ	**Tsade:** Signifies the end of a series, the finality of a period. The time when something has reached it's conclusion, is evaluated or judged and a new series begins. Nine is the last digit before a new number series begins

EXPLORING THE NUMERIC MEANING OF "THE EARTH"

In order to understand the numeric meaning of the Hebrew word "the Earth," you first need to understand the answer to the following question:

Did God create Adam and Eve perfect? Most people answer this question, yes.

Unfortunately, that is not the correct answer. Was Adam created perfect, or was he simply created sinless?

The importance of this question will become obvious as we continue exploring the numeric meaning of the Hebrew word "the Earth."

Genesis 2:18
And the LORD God said, It is not good that the man should be alone; I will make him an help meet for him."

There is a great mystery tucked into this little verse. Before we dive too deep into the meaning, let's glean the obvious.

Adam, who was acting at this point as the vice-regent of the entire Earth, after reviewing and naming all the animals that God put before him, concluded that among all God's creatures, there was not one that was suitable as a helper or companion for him.

God obviously already knew this, and the exercise was designed to inform Adam of this fact.

Adam was created with an insufficiency that created in Adam a condition that God said "was not good."

Genesis 2:18-22
And the LORD God said, It is not good that the man should be alone; I will make an help meet for him.

And out of the ground the LORD God formed every beast of the field, and every fowl of the air; and brought them unto Adam to see what he would call them: and whatsoever Adam called every living creature, that was the name thereof.

And Adam gave names to all cattle, and to

Bas relief on the facade of The Cathedral of Orvieto, Umbria, Italy, depicts the creation of Eve. Circa 1300

the fowl of the air, and to every beast of the field; but for Adam there was not found an help meet for him.

And the LORD God caused a deep sleep to fall upon Adam, and he slept: and he took one of his ribs, and closed up the flesh instead thereof;

And the rib, which the LORD God had taken from man, made he a woman, and brought her unto the man.

So what does this have to do with the Earth? Every drama needs a stage.

The Earth is not only our place of residence, it is an intricately designed, magnificently diverse and wondrously beautiful stage upon which we are living out the very tail end of a 6,000 year period that is enfolded into a 7,000 year drama.

If you're wondering what your part is in this drama – a drama in which you are both an actor and a spectator – a possible answer is forthcoming.

Bas relief on the facade of The Cathedral of Orvieto, Umbria, Italy, depicts the expulsion from Eden. Circa 1300

BACK TO SCENE ONE

In order to understand what is happening today on the Earth and the purpose of the Earth, you need to understand how this drama all began.

As you watch it unfold, perhaps some of life's biggest questions will be answered. It all started around 6,000 years ago in a Garden east of Eden.

One of the things I have heard repeated over and over again by Christians is that God created man for fellowship with Himself.

While I do not disagree, I do think this needs to be understood in a broader context that has been missing from this conversation.

Let's go back to scene one, where God formed Man out of the dust of the Earth and breathed into him the breath of life. Adam awoke to find himself literally in the hands of God his Creator, having received the kiss of life and the smiling approval of the Creator.

It was all declared to be very good and we are left to wonder if it could ever get any better.

The privileges given to Man were bountiful and wide-ranging, albeit unearned. His intellect was unsurpassed and unequaled.

But, as we read Man's early history, we find that Adam, in a flash of rebellion, would soon be returned in disgrace to the dust from which he was formed. Adam's body returned to the Earth.

The scene leaves one breathless and grasping for answers to questions that echo even into our present age.

Those who believe and esteem God's revelation of the genesis of Man have asked whether God's purpose for Man on the Earth was hijacked by malignant and malicious spiritual forces?

Was God outmaneuvered by the cunning and stealth of Satan? Was God caught by surprise and momentarily stunned by the hubris and boldness of His fallen creature, Lucifer?

Many Christians today are under the influence of this view, albeit modified to shade the obvious implication that God was surprised by the events that took place in the Garden of Eden.

I would ask you to consider another view. Is it not a reasonable assumption that God had an overarching purpose in all this drama that remains hidden amidst all the swirling chaos and confusion that has marked out Man's existence since that first fateful bite from the forbidden fruit? And while the implications of this hidden plan seem to elude us, we are driven by our faith and confidence in the wisdom and graciousness of God to always conclude that God is always good.

How we understand this can either undermine or bolster our confidence in God's good plans for us. So let's camp on this issue until we come to an understanding of *what in the world* this is all about.

WHAT IS THE PURPOSE OF MAN ON THIS EARTH?

Of all the systems that have been employed to try and organize the meaning of the ancient prophetic texts contained in what we call the Old and New Testament, there is but one that satisfies the literal interpretation of the Scriptures.

The system is called *dispensationalism*. And while it is not the purpose of this book to defend or refute this theological viewpoint, it does offer a frame-work for understanding the question that is before us. The primary point of the dispensational system can be summarized as follows: God has different ways of dealing with Man through history.

These *different ways or different economies* organize themselves progressively through time and history and culminate in a 1,000 year period called the Millennium.

The intervening periods of time, based on classical dispensationalism, generally fall into the following categories:

> **1. Innocence** (Genesis 1-3) - Adam and Eve before they sinned
> **2. Conscience** (Genesis 3-8) - First sin to the flood
> **3. Civil Government** (Genesis 9-11) - After the flood, government
> **4. Promise** (Genesis – Exodus 19) - Abraham to Moses, the Law is given
> **5. Law** (Exodus 20 – Acts 2:4) - Moses to the Cross
> **6. Grace** (Acts 2:4 – Revelation 20:3) - Cross to the Millennial Kingdom
> **7. Millennial Kingdom** (Revelation 20:4-6) - The rule of Christ on Earth, the Millennial Kingdom

It is not the purpose of this book to settle the debates that swirl around dispensational theology. My purpose is to borrow the classical dispensational architecture of the time periods – periods in which different governing principles were unquestionably in play – and suggest a reason for these different economies, a reason that overshadows everything else.

The trail marker for this quest is found in the pictorial meaning of the Hebrew word "the Earth." As a reminder:

> The purpose of the Earth is to reveal the

Creator, the Son of God who we are to behold and desire above all.

God has so ordered the footsteps of Mankind treading across Earth's stage to be introduced along the way to a wide range and diverse set of life-governing principles.

These situational lifestyles include everything from carefree Eden to the heavy-handed oppression and taxation that ultimately results from the governing schemes of kings, despots and dictators.

Man lived in an age of almost complete lawlessness before the flood of Noah, and Man has also lived in dispensations of time when laws and regulations subdued Man into a condition both paralyzing and hopeless.

Man has chaffed under the perfect regulating strictures of God's law, as given to Moses and, in his desire to be free from restraints, has sullied and debauched himself under the influence of lawless Pagan gods.

Within the seven dispensations mentioned here, there are sub-stratas of history. These vignettes offer up unique venues with their own insights into how Man responds to different philosophical and theological schemes of living.

The range is broad and rich with sad lessons – from the hermit's lonely existence to life in a commune directed by leaders – that mark the scale from witless to wicked. Man has experienced it all.

Even those most optimistic among us would have to agree that all of these experiments in governance seem guided by a golden gleam of hope but always end up in failure.

The closest thing to utopia is the promised and soon coming 1,000 year millennial reign of Jesus Christ on a restored Earth.

It promises to start stunningly well, but the same Scriptures that herald its magnificent beginning also forecast its calamitous and bloody ending.

If Earth is the stage upon which we are to not only value but desire with all our heart and mind and soul the Prince of Heaven, the Creator of Earth and the Savior of Mankind, then it should be no surprise that all the scenes played out through the sad and sorrowful history of Man should prepare us to embrace with a whole heart the Son of God. He is our only hope and our Savior.

The pictographic and numeric translations of the Hebrew word "the Earth" makes this clear.

And, just so the message is not lost, there is one letter in the Hebrew word "the Earth" that summarizes it succinctly.

REYSH

The second letter in the Hebrew word "the Earth" is reysh (hey is translated as "and," making reysh the second letter in the word "the Earth").

Reysh

The placement of the letter in the second position is a hint, a clue as to who the prince, the head man, is in the unique context of this word.

Is it not the second person of the Trinity, the Son of God?

The letter that follows reysh is the letter tsade, the fish hook and the pictogram that conveys the meaning of to strongly desire something or to be

hooked by it.

So the message is clear. We are to strongly desire the Son, who is the Messiah, the anointed Savior. He is our salvation!

There is an implied double meaning in the word savior. Someone needs to be saved!

The two concepts of savior and those needing salvation are obviously connected.

If no one needs salvation, a savior is of no value or importance.

If there is a great need for salvation but there is no savior, then tragically there is no hope of salvation.

In the context of the Hebrew word "the Earth," the second letter, reysh, is the Prince of Heaven come to Earth on a mission to save Mankind. That is the picture.

The number represented by reysh is 200. The number 200 is the number that signifies insufficiency. In the context of this revelation, the meaning is clear.

> The Savior (reysh) is on a mission to save the lost, those who cannot save themselves because they are insufficient for the task.

> The concept of savior and the condition of those being saved is revealed in the second letter of the Hebrew word for "the Earth."

The purpose of Earth is to play its part as a stage upon which each new scene opens with a scheme by which Man can perfect himself and demonstrate that he alone is sufficiently up to the task of renovation and redemption.

And each new scene ends in utter and complete failure. The failure is not meant to drive men to despair but just the opposite.

It is meant for Man to understand that he has been placed on this Earth to discover his insufficiency so that he might seek with all his heart and desire above everything else on Earth, the Son of God, his Savior.

PUTTING THE NUMBERS TOGETHER

God's (aleph and 1) amazing grace (5) solves the intractable problem of Man's insufficiency (200) with His sufficiency (aleph and 1).

At the appointed time (90) God healed the breach between Himself and sinful Man by anointing (aleph and tav) His own Son (reysh and aleph and tav) to do a work of spiritual perfection on the Earth.

This work was accomplished at the appointed time by means of an iron nail (vav).

Mankind is now divided into two groups: those who love the Earth with all its accommodations, treasures, pleasures, hopes, dreams and vanities (200) and those who love and desire (tsade) the Son of God (reysh) more than anything on Earth.

Pictographic translation

Complete reference table, pages 16-17

| Desire Him | Prince | God's | Behold |

Behold God's Prince Desire Him

Numeric translation

Complete reference table, pages 18-21

By grace God will deal with Man's insufficiency, bringing it to an end by the sacrifice of His Son.

The Ancient Mystery in 3d Revealed
As the Scriptures Unfolded in Time

The majesty and splendor of Earth with all its wonders is but a flickering shadow of the One who created Earth. The purpose of Earth is not Earth, the purpose of Earth is the One who made the Earth. Man has been corrupted as a result of his fallen nature. Man is spiritually dead, his mind darkened and his soul withered without any ability to rightly respond to the place that is right under his feet, the Earth. With Man's vision restored by God's renewing Spirit we see the Earth again as it was meant to be seen. The Earth is not only the place that sustains us but it also the place where God has put us so that we might see the boundless wonders of His creation under our feet and above our heads. That is meant to coax out of us a trembling heart that cries, "Lord, I desire to know You above all else, my Creator and my Lord, the Maker of Heaven and Earth!"

 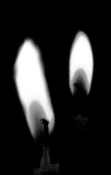 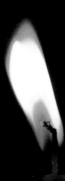 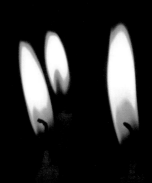

Chapter 10 – MYSTERIES REVEALED, PROPHECIES RESOLVED

God Left a Written Record of His Plan

The historical documentation of the message of redemption is yours to see.

A DASTARDLY DEED!

ALL the alarms in the cavernous headquarters went off at once. "What is happening?" shrieked the superintendent.

"Bedlam has broken out just outside Jerusalem," screamed one of the lieutenants. It was just then that reports began flooding in from all the agents stationed all around the Holy City.

"A crime of monumental proportions has just taken place in Bethany!" shouted one of the agents as he listened intently on his wireless for more breaking news.

The noise level in headquarters began steadily increasing and, finally, little could be heard above the din.

There was panic in the air that you could smell. There was the faint aroma of sulfur that rose into the atmosphere as the cavern boiled with anxiety.

Just then all went silent as a dark presence entered the cavern through the dimly lit corridor. The superintendent quickly neatened his desk as his hands began to shake. "Your majesty," he saluted as he stood at attention.

"What has just happened?" the creature menacingly demanded in tones just above a whisper.

"A dastardly deed!" the superintendent reported.

"What? What?" the Dark Prince impatiently snapped.

The superintendent lowered his eyes so as not to meet the icy glare of his master who towered above him menacingly.

"It's that man from Nazareth," the superintendent reported.

"Yes! Yes!" the Dark Prince boomed. The superintendent continued, "That man from Nazareth has just raised Lazarus of Bethany from the dead."

The Dark Prince took a step back and winced. For a few moments the room went ice cold and then heated up again as the Dark Prince regained his composure.

"This cannot be allowed to stand," the Prince barked. "Kill him! "Kill him now!" The Prince boomed as he pounded on the superintendent's desk.

"Lazarus?" queried the superintendent.

"Of course Lazarus," said the Prince, "And that other fellow also."

The superintendent straightened himself and asked meekly, "Jesus?"

No sooner had the name escaped his quivering lips than a torrent of shrieks and howls went out from the place like a tornado in a hayfield.

"Never, and I mean never, mention that name to me again!" the Dark Prince, now livid and animated, exclaimed.

The superintendent hurriedly changed the topic. "I will contact all our agents and put them on the case immediately" the superintendent confidently proclaimed.

The Dark Prince seemed unsatisfied with the answer. "Yes, put all our agents on the case, and put our best agents to work influencing the chief priests and scribes residing in Jerusalem."

With that settled, the Dark Prince slowly began stroking his chin in deep thought.

"Is there something else, Master?" asked the superintendent?

"Oh yes," the Dark Prince said, as his countenance lightened for a moment. " I have a friend among the Nazarene's disciples. It's time I pay him a visit."

THE LAST ENEMY

The raising of Lazarus was a small tremor that forecast an event so breathtakingly enormous that its aftershocks are felt to this day.

You can read about the raising of Lazarus of Bethany from the dead in the eleventh chapter of Luke.

Among the divinely appointed events recorded for us in order that we might believe in the name of Jesus the Christ, none is more poignant than the raising of Lazarus from the dead.

It was designed to take place just weeks before the resurrection from the dead of another man.

This event shook the gates of Hell off its hinges and broke the chains that had held it fast for millennia.

THE FINAL ENEMY

Death is the enemy. It is the final arbiter of Man's true condition. You might think that the act of raising a man from the dead would be cause for celebration and hope. And for some it was a happy event celebrated with joy and wonder.

But for others it was the event that heralded the death of the Messiah. Shorty after the raising of Lazarus the leadership of Israel went into a frenzy fearing that if Jesus were allowed to continue working His miraculous wonders that soon all Israel would follow Him.

This possibility was an affront to their leadership,

their livelihood, and their power base.

When Lazarus was raised from the dead the response from the chief priests and elders was to kill Lazarus. They also conspired to kill the man from Nazareth who had raised Lazarus from the dead.

Obviously this response was initiated from another realm of authority far beyond the physical leadership of Israel.

The response is Satanic in its very essence and cannot be understood without viewing it through that twisted lens of reality.

The principalities and powers and rulers of dark places were now pulling the strings, and pulling them hard. All the hosts of Hell soon joined the battle.

We are given a written record of how things really work in this fallen world.

The unveiling is shocking to some who have never considered the fact that this world is now occupied by entities that hate Mankind and work tirelessly to destroy it.

Matthew 26:3-4
Then assembled together the chief priests, and the scribes, and the elders of the people, unto the palace of the high priest, who was called Caiaphas, and consulted that they might take Jesus by subtlety, and kill him.

If Lazarus rising from the dead will not convince them, certainly Jesus the Christ raising Himself from the dead will. Don't count on it!

Jesus tells the true story of an un-named rich man and a poor beggar named Lazarus (not Lazarus of Bethany whom Jesus raised from the dead). The beggar Lazarus is laid outside the rich man's gate. Lazarus is covered with open sores. He is hungry and desires the crumbs from the rich mans table. Lazarus's companions are the dogs that lick his sores.

The rich man who lives a self-centered sumptuous lifestyle ignores Lazarus's considerable afflictions.

With the passage of time both men die.

The angels take Lazarus to Paradise and the rich man, who by tradition is named Dives, is taken to the place of torment.

Abraham is in Paradise, separated by a wide gulf from the place of torment. From across this gulf Dives engages Abraham in a conversation.

Dives first requests that his suffering be relieved. Abraham denies his plea for two reasons. One is based on the irreversible and finality of the sentence of justice. The other reason is based on Dives' location in Hell. Dives is in a place separated from Abraham by a wide gulf that cannot be traversed.

The second request of Dives is that Lazarus be allowed to return to Earth as one who has risen from the dead. Dives desires that Lazarus return to warn his five brothers to repent.

Dives wants his brothers to avoid his hellish fate. It seems a selfless request. The request is denied. Listen to the response of Abraham as quoted by Jesus.

Luke 16:29-31
Abraham saith unto him, they have Moses and the prophets; let them hear them. And he said, Nay, father Abraham: but if one went unto them from the dead, they will repent. And he said unto him, if they hear not Moses and the prophets, neither will they be persuaded, though one rose from the dead.

HE IS RISEN!

With this story in our minds let's investigate the events that took place three days and three nights after the crucifixion of Jesus.

Matthew 28:5-7
And the angel answered and said unto the women, Fear not ye: for I know that ye seek Jesus, which was crucified. He is not here: for he is risen, as he said. Come, see the place where the Lord lay. And go quickly, and tell his disciples that ee is risen from the dead;

THE ANCIENT PROPHECY IS FULLFILLED

Who was the first person to see the risen Christ? Is it surprising that the answer is Mary Magdalene?

Few have bothered to think very deeply about why it was a woman who was the first to see Messiah after His bodily resurrection.

Mary Magdalene is not just any woman; she is a woman with a sad and sinful past, a notorious sinner.

Nothing about the life, death, burial, and resurrection of Jesus happened without a divine purpose. There is a spiritual order to the events that God has ordained for His own glory.

In this instance, God has allowed us to view it so that we might be instructed and gain wisdom.

Let's take a few minutes and deconstruct the events immediately following the glorious resurrection of Jesus the Christ.

Perhaps we will glimpse the crimson thread of the Word revealing Himself in the events that took place after His resurrection.

The resurrection of the Messiah prophetically fulfilled and sealed a promise that had been made to a woman more than 4,000 years earlier.

This covenant promise was the foundation stone upon which all other prophecy found in the ancient Scriptures rested.

It was the unconditional promise that a Savior would one day come from the seed of a woman to redeem fallen Mankind (Genesis 3:15).

Why was Mary Magdalene chosen by God as the first person to see the risen Savior?

> Remember that the first person to receive the first prophecy upon which the salvation of all Mankind depended was a woman.

> Eve received the promise. It was a promise that from her seed a Deliverer would come forth.

Mary Magdalene stands out in the Scriptures, and was declared by Jesus to be the example of those that "loved much."

You can read the account in the Gospel of Luke, chapter seven, starting at verse 36.

It was to this woman, Mary Magdalene, that Jesus said, "Thy sins are forgiven."

Mary Magdalene, who was a great sinner before the Lord forgave her, stands out in bold relief as the perfect picture of the truly redeemed.

Her response was an abiding, ever increasing, and overwhelming sense of gratitude.

Notice the inkblot symmetry in the glorious fulfillment of God's promises. It is truly amazing!

Christus relurgens apparet Marie Magdalenæ

THE DUSTY ROAD FROM CREATION TO REDEMPTION

After appearing to Mary Magdalene you might imagine that Jesus would appear to His eleven disciples. But instead Jesus does something unexpected, wonderful, and very instructive.

Before the risen Savior makes Himself known to the eleven, He has a mission that takes Him to a dusty road just outside of Jerusalem.

It is while treading the dirt pathway just outside of Jerusalem that He strikes up a conversation with two of His disciples.

These two disciples are not among the eleven. One of the disciples is identified as Cleopas, believed to be the uncle of Jesus. It follows then, that the other disciple was in all likelihood the wife of Cleopas.

These two disciples would have recognized Jesus anywhere. Why was His identity hidden from them? This seems to be a mystery.

Something important needs to take place before the physical profile of the risen Lord is revealed to these two loving disciples of Jesus.

There is a path that must be patiently traversed before the physical resurrection of Jesus is disclosed to these favored followers of the Messiah. It is a journey through the ancient prophetic Scriptures.

Before they were given physical eyes to see the Messiah they must first have their hearts and minds instructed and informed by the Living Word. It is only through spiritual eyes that we can fully understand and appreciate the wonders of our Redeemer.

What is the pre-eminent revelation that precedes the actual disclosure of the risen Messiah? Thankfully the outline of it is carefully preserved and recorded for us?

You can read the words of Jesus as recorded in the twenty-fifth chapter of the Gospel of Luke to discover the answer.

Luke 24:25-27
Then he said unto them, O fools, and slow of heart to believe all that the prophets have spoken: Ought not Christ to have suffered these things, and to enter into his glory?

And beginning at Moses and all the prophets, he expounded unto them in all the scriptures the things concerning himself.

This is astonishing! The risen Savior hides His identity from His own disciples in order to paint for them His own portrait.

The risen Savior uses a brush laden with Scripture, drawing upon the prophetic palette the primary colors of promise and expectation. The result is no muddled collage. It is a finely detailed depiction of the suffering and saving Messiah.

Do you want to view the Savior? Do you desire to know and understand Him? Do you know where to begin your search?

According to the Lord Himself the journey starts in the first book of the Scriptures.

Can the Messiah be found in the first book in the Torah written by Moses? Jesus thought so! The Lord began His own self-disclosure in the book of Genesis. Do you wish to progress further in your understanding of the Messiah? Read the prophets.

This is the pattern and example of how the Messiah might be found. A pattern both initiated and recommended by the Messiah Himself. See John 5:39.

Can you imagine with me the sermon that Jesus preached to His two attentive disciples as they slowly walked to the small village of Emmaus?

The Scriptures tell us that Jesus expounded *all* the Scriptures that contained things concerning Himself. This was no three-minute sermonette.

Jesus took these two disciples whom He loved on a lengthy and exhaustive journey through the written Word. This journey must have taken place over many hours.

It would be impossible to replicate the precise sermon that Jesus preached.

While we cannot know exactly what the Lord disclosed regarding Himself we can roughly outline the Lord's revelation.

Gospel evangelists have exercised the prophecies revealing the Messiah for two thousand years. We would be wise not to stray from this path and pattern of evangelism.

Let's see if we can reconstruct the sermon that set his two disciples hearts on fire.

Luke 24: 32
And they said one to another,
Did not our heart burn within us,
While he talked with us by the way,
And while he opened to us the scriptures?

Did Jesus start by reminding them of the promise given to Eve as it was recorded in Genesis?

Genesis 3:15
And I will put enmity between thee and the woman, And between thy seed and her seed;

It shall bruise thy head, and thou shalt bruise his heel.

Did the Messiah share with them the story of the brazen serpent that Moses lifted up on a pole in the wilderness?

Numbers 21:9
And Moses made a serpent of brass,
And put it upon a pole, and it came to pass,
That if a serpent had bitten any man,
When he beheld the serpent of brass, He lived.

Can you hear the Savior explaining as he did to Nicodemus the meaning of the brass serpent hanging on the pole?

John 3:14-15
And as Moses lifted up the serpent in the wilderness, Even so must the Son of man be lifted up:
That whosoever believeth in him
Should not perish, but have eternal life.

I have little doubt that Jesus quoted the prophet Isaiah.

Can you hear Him asking His two disciples if they understood that the prophet Isaiah was speaking of the Messiah?

Isaiah 53:3
He is despised and rejected of men; A man of sorrows, And acquainted with grief:

Isaiah 53:4
Surely he hath borne our griefs, And carried our sorrows:

Isaiah 53:5
But he was wounded for our transgressions, He was bruised for our iniquities:

Isaiah 53:5b
And with his stripes we are healed.

Isaiah 53:6b
The Lord hath laid on him the iniquity of us all.

Isaiah 53:7
He was oppressed, and he was afflicted, Yet he opened not his mouth:

Isaiah 53:8b
He was cut off out of the land of the living: for the transgression of my people was he stricken.

Isaiah 53:9
And he made his grave with the wicked, and with the rich in his death;

Isaiah 53:10b
When thou shalt make his soul An offering for sin,

Isaiah 53:12b
And he bare the sin of many, and made intercession for the transgressors.

Imagine Jesus reminding His disciples that the very words the Messiah spoke from the cross and the events that took place under His pierced heels were direct quotes and prophesies found in the ancient book of the Psalms of King David?

Psalms 22:1
My God, my God, why hast thou forsaken me?

Psalms 22:7-8
All they that see me laugh me to scorn: they shoot out the lip, they shake the head, saying, He trusted on the Lord that he would deliver him: Let him deliver him

Psalms 22:14
I am poured out like water, and all my bones are out of joint: my heart is like wax; it is melted in the midst of my bowels.

Psalms 22:16b
…They pierced my hands and my feet.

Psalms 22:18
They part my garments among them, and cast lots upon my vesture.

Did Jesus ask them where Micah prophesied the Messiah would be born? As relatives of Jesus they would have known that He was born in Bethlehem.

Micah 5:2
But thou, Bethlehem Ephratah, though thou be little among the thousands of Judah, yet out of thee shall he come forth unto me that is to be ruler in Israel; whose goings forth have been from of old, from everlasting.

As Jesus expounded on the things concerning Himself as recorded by Moses and the prophets He probably included the following (first verse reference is the prophecy, second is the fulfillment).

Jeremiah prophesied that the Messiah would be a descendent of David.
Jeremiah 23:5-6 – Luke 3:23-31

Daniel prophesied that the Messiah would present Himself exactly 483 years after the decree went out from Artaxerxes to rebuild the city of Jerusalem. Jesus had fulfilled that prophecy on the 10th of Nisan 32 AD. Just 6 or 7 days earlier.
Daniel 9:25 – John 12: 12-13

Isaiah prophesied that the Messiah would begin His ministry in Galilee.
Isaiah 9:1,2 – Matthew 4:12-17

King David prophesied that the Messiah would teach in parables.

    Psalms 78:1-2

Zechariah prophesied that the Messiah would have a ministry to the poor and humble believing remnant.

    Zechariah 11:7 – Matthew 9:35-36

Jeremiah and Isaiah prophesied that the Messiah Would be born of a virgin.

    Isaiah 7:14, Jeremiah 31:22, –
    Matthew 1:18-20, Luke 1:35

Isaiah prophesied that the Messiah would be known as a Nazarene.

    Isaiah 11:1 – Matthew 2:23

Haggai prophesied that the Messiah would visit the second Temple.

    Haggai 2:6-9 – Luke 2:27-32

Zechariah prophesied that the Messiah would be heralded as a King and would ride a donkey into Jerusalem.

    Zechariah 9:9 - John 12:12-13

King David and Zechariah both prophesied that the Messiah would be betrayed by a friend for 30 pieces of silver and He would confront His enemies in a garden.

    Psalms 41:9, Psalms 55:12-14
    Zechariah 11:12-13,
    Psalms 40:14 - John 18:4-6
    Matthew 26:14-15, John 13:18

King David prophesied that the Messiah would suffer an agonizing violent death.

    Psalms 22:14,15, Zechariah 13:7
    Matthew 15:34-37, Matthew 27:35

There are more than 300 specific prophecies and fulfillments regarding the Messiah generously sprinkled throughout the books of Moses and the prophets. I have included only a few.

Five years ago I would end this chapter with the true but woefully understated estimate that "more than 300 specific" prophecies regarding Messiah are to be found in the ancient prophetic text. Based on what I know now the only question is how many zeros to add to the number 300. Should I add one, ten, a hundred or more?

If I had asked you the following question before you took up this little book and read it, what would have been your answer?

How many Messianic prophetic harbingers are in the first verse of the ancient Scriptures?

Can you find the Messiah in the 28 Hebrew letters that make up the five words declared in Genesis 1:1?

The astute among you might make the connection between John 1:1-3 and Genesis 1:1 and answer *one*.

So how many Messianic prophecies and references are there in Genesis 1:1?

The honest answer is that I cannot know or ever fully know the answer to this question. I have discovered dozens and will now share a sampling from that list. This is obviously just the tip of the proverbial iceberg.

There are letter/pictures and letter/numbers embedded in the ancient prophetic Scriptures that are beyond my understanding. One day perhaps the Lord will graciously unveil the corners of this generous and borderless mystery to me.

I look forward to that day of discovery!

SUMMARY OF
MESSIANIC HARBINGERS
HIDDEN IN PLAIN SIGHT

In the very first word found in the Scriptures we have the following pre-eminent prophetic disclosures.

I will rehearse and summarize them for your consideration.

To remind you of the details regarding these revelations simply refer to them as they are found in this book.

IN BEGINNING

1. The pictographic message: The Son of God Pressed by His Own Hand to a Cross

2. The numeric message: In the letter/number Yood and Tav we have the only two numbers that are directly connected to Time.

Yood (a deed) = 10 Tav (the cross) = 400

The great deed to be accomplished on a cross will begin in 4000 years (10x400)

3. The pictographic and numeric message: Man cannot save himself and is insufficient and unable to accomplish his own deliverance from sin and death.

God's Son will accomplish by miraculous means the victory over sin and death resulting in the restoration and salvation of Mankind

In the second word in the Scriptures we have the following pre-eminent prophetic disclosures.

HE CREATED

4. The pictographic message: The second word in ancient Scriptures gives us the identity of the One who is in the beginning creating. It is He whose hands will be pressed against a cross.

It is The Son of God!

5. The numeric message: The second word is a message full of home for fallen Man.

The Son of God overcomes Man's insufficiency with His all sufficiency!

In the third word in the Scriptures we have the following pre-eminent prophetic disclosures.

ELOHIM

6. The numeric message: God the Father will bring about deliverance through His Anointed One.

At the divinely ordained time He will bring about the revival and renewal of Man by His grace.

In the fourth un-translated word in the Scriptures we have the following pre-eminent prophetic disclosures.

THE ALEPH AND TAV

7. The pictographic message: The strong leader will make a covenant guaranteed by the sign of the cross.

8. The pictographic and numeric message: Messiah is the Alpha and the Omega, the First and the Last, the Beginning and the End.

9. The conventional message: Jesus is the entire Word from Aleph to Tav (A to Z)

In the fifth word in the Scriptures we have the following pre-eminent prophetic disclosures.

THE HEAVENS

10. The numeric message: There will be a time of testing for Mankind that will demonstrate his utter inability to save himself.

God's grace accomplished by a mighty deed will accomplish something that Man cannot accomplish for himself – divine restoration and salvation.

In the last word found in Genesis 1:1 we have the following pre-eminent prophetic disclosures.

THE EARTH

11. The pictographic message: Behold God's Son and desire Him!

12. The numeric message: The sacrifice of God's Son will finally bring to an end the covenant of sin and death that Man has entered into.

God will graciously deal with Man's insufficiency.

Incredibly in the first 28 letters we have a dozen Messianic prophetic harbingers.

Are there more hidden in plain sight? Let's take a look.

THE MYSTERY OF THE NUMBER 28 THE LAST LETTER IN GENESIS 1:1

There are 28 letters in the first verse in Genesis 1:1. The number 28 means creation – spiritual perfection – eternal life

The 28th letter, tsade, sums up the essence of Genesis 1:1. Genesis 1:1 is a revelation designed to create a *desire* for the Son of God!

There is a miracle in the number placement of the first verse in the Scriptures that is designed to illuminate the redemptive architecture that God has revealed down to the letter!

THE MYSTERY OF THE MIDDLE LETTER

Both ancient and modern Rabbis have noticed that the essence, or key, to understanding a Hebrew word is often found in the meaning of the letter that is in the middle of the word. We have also discovered this to be true

There are three Hebrew words found in Genesis 1:1 that have a single middle letter. They are as follows:

HE CREATED

The Prince
(middle letter)

ELOHIM

אלהים

Reveals
(middle letter)

THE HEAVENS

השמים

The Waters
(middle letter)

There are *five* revelations in this disclosure.

The first: He Created
The first is that the One who did the creating is identified as the Prince of Heaven, the Son of God.

The second: Elohim
The second disclosure is that God is the One who does the revealing.

The third: The Heavens
The third disclosure is that the Son of God describes the heavens as the place where Man will ultimately experience the life that results from drinking the life-giving water offered.

The Fourth: When you put the three letters together you get the following pictographic and numeric message:

The Prince (the Son of God) Reveals the Waters (of Life).

ר.ה.מ

The Fifth: When you put the three letters together you get the following numeric message:

Man has been (40) tested and found (200) insufficient to accomplish his own salvation.

What Man cannot achieve, the Son of God has achieved at Calvary – (40) resurrection and renewal.

The gift of eternal life has been freely and (5) graciously offered to all Mankind.

THE MESSIANIC MYSTERY OF THE EIGHT: ETERNAL LIFE

We discovered in Chapter Three that beyt-reysh-aleph as a pictogram declared that the "He" who "created" all things was The Son Of God.

The pictograms behind the Hebrew letters beyt reysh is the Prince coming out of the tent or house. In other words The Son.

The Prince being pictured in the eighth letter in the Hebrew Scriptures is none other than The Prince of Heaven who is the King of Heaven (God the Father's) Only Begotten Son.

The number eight crowns the head of the Prince as it stands over reysh as the eighth letter revealed in the Torah.

Eight has a very special meaning. Eight means eternality or eternal life. So here we have the imbedded message that:

The Prince of Heaven holds the keys to eternal life.

John 17:3
And this is life eternal, that they might know thee the only true God, and Jesus Christ, whom thou hast sent.

HALF THE TREASURE MAP!

There is an old saying that most of you have probably heard. It goes like this:

The New is in the Old concealed, and
the Old is in the New revealed.

There is a story of two brothers who each received half of a treasure map.

Without both halves the treasure would remain hidden. It was not until the two halves were joined that the location of their inherited treasure might be found.

MYSTERY OF THE TORAH LETTERS

Do you know how many letters there are in the entirety of the Books of Moses, otherwise known as the Torah – the first five books of the Bible?

The mystic rabbis claimed that there were 600,000 letters. Thanks to the computer age we can verify that this is incorrect. There are *exactly* 304,805 letters in the Torah. Above are the top three letters as they appear in the Torah arranged in descending order based on the number of times each letter is used in the Torah. Now let's look at

No. of times found in Torah		Number - Letter	Pictogram
28,052	ה	5 - hey	behold
30,509	ו	6 - vav	iron nail
31,522	י	10 - yood	hand

Pictographic message based on the top three letters found in the Torah:

ה ו י

yood - vav - hey

Behold the hand and the nail!

Numeric message based on the top three letters found in the Torah:

No. of times found in Torah		Number - Letter	Meaning
28,052	ה	5 - hey	grace
30,509	ו	6 - vav	Man
31,522	י	10 - yood	ordinal perfection

ה ו י

10 - 6 - 5

(10) In God's perfect time and according to His plan (5) God showed grace to fallen Man

---

the message based on the bottom three letters used in the Torah:

John 3:14-15

And as Moses lifted up the serpent in the wilderness, even so must the Son of man be lifted up: That whosoever believeth in him should not perish, but have eternal life.

ACCORDING TO THE SCRIPTURES!

If you read the New Testament carefully you will notice an interesting statement that shows up over and over again. The recurring statement is "according to the Scriptures" or "as it is written." The events and actual geographical locations surrounding the life, ministry, death, and resurrection of Jesus the Christ are chronicled in the Gospels of Matthew, Mark, Luke and John.

These events and locations were forecast in the written testimony of the ancient prophetic text we call the Old Testament.

In some cases these prophecies were written five hundred years before the actual event took place. In many cases they were forecast over a thousand years before they manifested in time and space. In addition to places and events being forecast, actual time stamps were published hundreds of years in advance of the heralded event.

The prophet Daniel forecast that the Messiah would announce Himself in the year 32 AD on Nisan 10. The only candidate for the fulfillment of this prophecy was Jesus. The date 32 AD has come and gone and you are left with only one bona-fide candidate.

The purpose of this book is to introduce you to the one and only Son of God, Savior and Redeemer of Mankind. His name is Yeshua Ha-Mashiach aka Jesus the Christ. The simple point is that God left a written record of how His redemptive plan was going to take place, including information about when and where it would unfold.

The evidence is now increasing in these final days.

No. of times found in Torah	Number - Letter	Pictogram
1,802	ט 9 - tet	snake
1,833	ס 15 - samech	prop up
2,109	ג 3- gimel	camel

ג ס ט

to lift up - pole to support - surround

Lift up the serpent on the pole

I find it astounding that Yeshua Ha-Mashiach aka Jesus the Christ is hidden in plain sight in the very Hebrew letters and numbers of the ancient prophetic Scriptures.

Ancient did I say? Ancient implies a dusty corroded relic from the past, but I can assure you that this is not the case. The Ancient of Days is an accurate description of what we come in contact with when we read the ancient prophetic texts through the eyes of faith and with the aid of God Himself. Our current hope is based on ancient promises made by Someone more ancient than the promises themselves. He is ancient but He is not remote. He is alive and lives at the right hand of God the Father making intercession for all that call upon His name in faith.

Question: And why is this possible?
Answer: The Ancient Word became flesh and dwelt among us.
Question: How do we know?
Answer: The certain Word, the Living Word, and the Living Word in 3D declares it to be so.

The information I have uncovered can be added to the already overwhelming historical record of the early and often repeated message of redemption that God placed within Mankind's reach.

FINAL 3-D SUMMARY OF GENESIS 1:1 FROM THE PERSPECTIVE OF CALVARY

Calvary is the Key that Unlocks The Gospel in Genesis 1:1. The Son of God, Who was in the beginning creating the heavens and the Earth, also knew what would happen in the end.

He knew that the Man He had fashioned sinless with His own hands out of the red Earth would deliberately fall out of fellowship with Him. He knew that the descent into sin and rebellion left unremedied would forever banish Man from His presence. He knew that the consequences of Man's fall from grace would sadly and finally end in Hell.

Knowing this to be the outcome, God fashioned a gracious plan designed to redeem Man. But first Man must be tested in order to demonstrate to him his weakness and insufficiency.

The path that would lead to restoration and eternal life was not an easy one for Man. But consider this – it was excruciatingly painful and extravagantly expensive for the Redeemer of Man.

It is true that the doorway to deliverance was meant to demonstrate to Man the seriousness and vile nature of his sin. It is a grander truth that was meant to demonstrate to Man the great love that the Son of God has for Mankind. He would endure Hell so that we might experience Heaven.

The Son of God suffered this anguish joyfully in order that we might be finally and eternally found in the embrace of His love and care.

Think about it!

Hebrews 12:2

Looking unto Jesus the author and finisher

of our faith; who for the joy that was set

before him endured the cross, despising the

shame, and is set down at the right hand

of the throne of God.

Epilogue – His Word and You

With God, There are No Random Events

How did this little book get into your hands? And why?

THANK you for taking the time to read this little book. I wonder if you might consider that the very fact that you have read this book has some deeper eternal purpose?

I hope you have been convincingly introduced to the fact that God has embedded His love story into the very letters and numbers of His Word.

Imagine the mastery over time and space that must have been a prerequisite for such a revelation to unfold with perfect precision.

Now imagine all the events that make up your personal reality. Is there a hidden hand guiding your destiny? Do you hear the drumbeat of circumstances in your life that continually re-orients your attention toward the Lord Jesus Christ?

The red arrow inside the compass cannot help but point to true North.

Is there a compass in your heart that keeps twisting you and moving you in the direction of the Savior and His cross?

There is a personal, loving intelligence at work in the universe, a gentle wind that blows the frail ships of men's lives into the safe harbors of the Savior's arms.

Lonely, angry, bitter, cynical, depressed, wounded and lost men have discovered to their utter amazement that a plan for their restoration is as near to them as a prayer whispered in the dark.

Is it conceivable that God would move Heaven and Earth in order that those He had set His heart on might read His story of love and sacrifice?

The Word that became flesh is also able by a miracle that only God fully understands to take up residence within you.

He has a book to write with your name on it. It is the book that chronicles your faith in Him.

The risen Lord Himself promises to author your book from the first word in the first chapter to the last word in the final chapter.

The God that created the Cosmos promises to dwell in those who receive the gift He offers on the basis of what He accomplished on your behalf by his life, death, burial, and resurrection.

He lives now at the right hand of God the Father.

He intercedes on your behalf so that you might one day be with Him forever.

Question: And what must you do to be saved?

Answer: Believe in the Lord Jesus the Christ and you will be saved!

Jesus comforted those He came to redeem with the following words. Is He speaking these words to you?

John 14:1-3
Let not your heart be troubled: ye believe in God believe also in me. In my Father's house are many mansions: if it were not so, I would have told you. I go to prepare a place for you. And if I go and prepare a place for you, I will come again, and receive you unto myself; that where I am, there ye may be also.

The sinner's prayer should always begin with this simple plea.

Lord reveal yourself to me!

The summary of what this is all about can be found in the lyrics of this old hymn:

TELL ME THE OLD, OLD STORY

A. Katherine Hankey, 1866

Tell me the old, old story of unseen things above,

Of Jesus and His glory, of Jesus and His love.

Tell me the story simply, as to a little child,

For I am weak and weary, and helpless and defiled.

Tell me the old, old story, tell me the old, old story,

Tell me the old, old story, of Jesus and His love.

Tell me the same old story when you have cause to fear

That this world's empty glory is costing me too dear.

Yes, and when that world's glory is dawning on my soul,

Tell me the old, old story: "Christ Jesus makes thee whole."

THE END

The Son of God
pressed by His own
hand to a cross

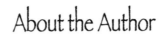

About the Author

C. J. Lovik graduated from Westmont College California with a degree in Education and Communication and taught elementary school in Southern California.

After teaching and writing children's books for many years, he started a manufacturing business and developed an online family-friendly internet search engine.

An edited and updated version of John Bunyan's classic, The Pilgrim's Progress: From This World to That Which Is to Come, published in 2009, was C.J.'s first book for adults.

His purpose in publishing this edition, was, in his own words, "To carry forward this treasured legacy for a new generation. With this as the objective, the text of this edition has only been lightly edited—to update archaic words and difficult sentence structure, while retaining the beauty and brilliance of the original story, and to let the story unfold with all the power, truth, and remarkable creativity of the original."

In 2004, C.J. produced an eight-part website, The Story of Jesus, that combines the four biographies written by Matthew, Mark, Luke and John into a single story line. The site has been viewed by untold thousands, many of whom were encountering the story of Jesus for the first time. The site remains busy today.

Acknowledgments

I would like to thank Tina Miller for her work as my editor, Adam Johnson for his inspired cover art, Dr. Chuck Missler, Jonathan Cahn and Gary Stearman for inspiring me, Dr. Danny Ben-Gigi for his expertise with the Hebrew language and for his help in getting everything going in the right direction, and Steve Stinson for the book's layout and design.

I would also like to acknowledge the indispensable works of E.W. Bullinger – *Number in Scripture,* Ed F. Vallowe – *Biblical Mathematics and Keys to Scripture Numerics,* and Dr. Frank T. Seekins – *Hebrew Word Pictures.*

All Bible verses in this book conform to
The Official King James Bible, Cambridge Edition
They can be referenced at:
www.kingjamesbibleonline.org

www.rockislandbooks.com

Visit our website to purchase books and preview upcoming titles.

Contact us at:
books@rockisland.com